Young

2004 POETRY C

# ONCE UPON A RHYME

# A RHYME

## IMAGINATION FOR
## A NEW GENERATION

# Poems From Surrey
### Edited by Steve Twelvetree

 Young**Writers**

First published in Great Britain in 2005 by:
Young Writers
Remus House
Coltsfoot Drive
Peterborough
PE2 9JX
Telephone: 01733 890066
Website: www.youngwriters.co.uk

SB ISBN 1 84460 677 5

# Foreword

Young Writers was established in 1991 and has been passionately devoted to the promotion of reading and writing in children and young adults ever since. The quest continues today. Young Writers remains as committed to engendering the fostering of burgeoning poetic and literary talent as ever.

This year's Young Writers competition has proven as vibrant and dynamic as ever and we are delighted to present a showcase of the best poetry from across the UK. Each poem has been carefully selected from a wealth of *Once Upon A Rhyme* entries before ultimately being published in this, our twelfth primary school poetry series.

Once again, we have been supremely impressed by the overall high quality of the entries we have received. The imagination, energy and creativity which has gone into each young writer's entry made choosing the best poems a challenging and often difficult but ultimately hugely rewarding task - the general high standard of the work submitted amply vindicating this opportunity to bring their poetry to a larger appreciative audience.

We sincerely hope you are pleased with our final selection and that you will enjoy *Once Upon A Rhyme Poems From Surrey* for many years to come.

# Contents

| | |
|---|---|
| Jack Bates  (10) | 74 |
| Beth Leahy  (10) | 74 |
| Chloë Brandon  (10) | 75 |
| Ellie Bissell  (10) | 75 |
| Scott Brown  (10) | 75 |

**Danes Hill School**

| | |
|---|---|
| Alice Jeffers  (10) | 76 |
| Sally Park  (10) | 77 |
| Will Elbourne  (10) | 77 |
| Laura Galloway  (10) | 78 |
| Thomas Eckl  (10) | 78 |
| Alexandra Smith  (10) | 79 |
| Emma Reynolds  (10) | 79 |
| George Brighton  (10) | 80 |
| Ben Allchurch  (10) | 80 |
| Domenyk Turski  (10) | 81 |
| John McNally  (10) | 82 |
| Adam Dayan  (10) | 82 |
| Katharine Burnett  (10) | 83 |
| Katelyn Aitchison  (11) | 84 |
| Catherine Keey  (10) | 84 |
| Laura Koepke  (10) | 85 |
| Catherine Thynne  (10) | 85 |
| George Rexstrew  (10) | 86 |
| Lucy Barrett  (10) | 86 |
| Isabelle Griffin  (10) | 87 |
| Balraj Gill  (10) | 88 |
| George Parry  (10) | 88 |
| Alexander Hurley  (10) | 89 |
| Abigail Lawrence  (10) | 90 |
| Kieran Copley  (10) | 91 |
| Nadia McLurcan  (10) | 92 |
| Sophie Vos  (10) | 93 |

**Ewell Castle Junior School**

| | |
|---|---|
| Edward Barton  (10) | 93 |
| Fred Kearey  (10) | 94 |
| Oliver Stansfield  (10) | 94 |
| Gregory Hughes  (10) | 95 |
| Sam Anderson  (10) | 95 |

| | |
|---|---|
| Sebastian Nowell (10) | 96 |
| Max Northfield (10) | 96 |
| Ismet Erdogan (10) | 97 |

## Goldsworth Primary School

| | |
|---|---|
| Nadeem Hussain (7) | 97 |
| Marion Stuttaford (7) | 98 |
| Mark Thornborrow (7) | 98 |
| Nathan Guy (7) | 98 |
| Katie Marriott (7) | 99 |
| Ben Morrant (8) | 99 |
| Jordan Appleyard (8) | 99 |
| Addison Bray (8) | 100 |
| Abigail Mattingly (7) | 100 |
| Amy Pearce (7) | 100 |
| Ruaridh Wallace (7) | 101 |
| Alice Saunders (7) | 101 |
| Sammy King (7) | 101 |

## Manor House School

| | |
|---|---|
| Sophie Jones (9) | 102 |
| Laura Bushnell (11) | 102 |
| Emily Williams (10) | 102 |
| Amber Hearns (9) | 103 |
| Maisie McCulloch (9) | 103 |
| Florence Mills (10) | 104 |
| Charlotte Ladd (11) | 104 |
| Georgia Bean (10) | 105 |
| Maddie Mortimore (10) | 105 |
| Lucy Sharples (10) | 106 |
| Komal Patel (10) | 106 |
| Megan Laura Day (11) | 107 |
| Elinor Abraham (10) | 107 |
| Katie Gilbard (10) | 108 |
| Rachel Swatman (10) | 108 |

## Marist RC Primary School

| | |
|---|---|
| Georgia Clark (8) | 109 |
| Charlotte Louise Manser (8) | 109 |
| Marianna Difelice (8) | 110 |
| Haydn Robinson (7) | 110 |

| | |
|---|---|
| Oliver Thompson  (7) | 146 |
| Sacha Femandes  (9) | 146 |
| Ashley Rannie  (8) | 147 |
| Max Brown  (9) | 147 |
| Susan Shiel-Rankin  (9) | 148 |
| Pietra Morello  (9) | 148 |
| Jack Rundle  (9) | 148 |
| Ella Worsfold  (9) | 149 |
| Isabelle Hurl  (9) | 149 |
| Billy Robbins | 149 |
| Rosalba Morello  (9) | 149 |
| Samuel Glennon  (9) | 150 |

**Nutfield Church CE Primary School**

| | |
|---|---|
| Emily Gay  (9) | 150 |
| Luke Bellars  (9) | 150 |
| Olivia Felton  (9) | 151 |
| Barnaby Yeldham  (10) | 151 |
| Ted Winder  (9) | 151 |
| Charlie Dowden  (9) | 152 |
| Jack Mighall  (9) | 152 |
| Jack Bellars  (10) | 153 |
| Joel Kemp  (10) | 153 |
| Maisy Wyer  (10) | 154 |
| Marnie McAdam  (9) | 154 |
| Dominic Harvey  (10) | 155 |
| Katie Richardson  (10) | 155 |
| Evangeline Foster  (10) | 156 |
| Caitlin Fine  (10) | 157 |
| Lily Donovan  (9) | 158 |

**Park Hill School**

| | |
|---|---|
| Ye-Rin Park  (9) | 158 |
| Jack Onslow  (10) | 159 |
| Tabitha Wallace  (10) | 159 |
| Jessica Hafenrichter  (10) | 160 |
| Antonia Harrison  (10) | 160 |
| Jaimie Freeman  (9) | 161 |
| Antonia Adams  (9) | 161 |
| Rebecca Anker  (9) | 162 |
| Ellie Nearchou  (11) | 162 |

## Parkside School

## Reigate Priory School

| | |
|---|---|
| William Franks  (10) | 181 |
| Sophie Mamalis  (8) | 181 |
| Athavan Bosch  (8) | 182 |
| Beth Alderman  (8) | 182 |
| Polly Griffiths  (8) | 183 |
| Max Anderson  (8) | 183 |
| Lucy Pullinger  (9) | 184 |
| Beth Craske  (8) | 184 |

## St Agatha's Catholic Primary School, Kingston-upon-Thames

| | |
|---|---|
| Soracha Healy  (10) | 185 |
| Sophie Dowsett  (10) | 185 |
| Conor McGovern-Paul  (8) | 186 |
| Vanessa Adofo  (8) | 186 |
| Christina Paish  (8) | 187 |
| Eleanor O'Leary  (8) | 187 |
| Natalia Jezierski  (10) | 188 |
| Josef James  (8) | 188 |
| Luke Pearce  (8) | 189 |
| Caitlin King  (8) | 189 |
| Danielle Hernandez  (8) | 190 |
| Daniela Cavallino  (8) | 190 |
| Amber Kijowski  (8) | 191 |
| Fiona Kitchen  (8) | 191 |

## St John's Primary School, Woking

| | |
|---|---|
| Dasha Barsky  (10) | 192 |
| Elizabeth Westmacott  (9) | 192 |
| Cameron Purdie  (9) | 192 |
| Jake Powell  (10) | 193 |
| Jennifer Atkinson  (9) | 193 |
| Billy Hack  (9) | 193 |
| Megan Oakley  (10) | 194 |
| Josie Pullen  (9) | 194 |
| Georgia Compton  (9) | 194 |
| Stephen Nicholls  (10) | 195 |
| Katie Jane Taggart  (10) | 195 |
| Michael Gent  (10) | 195 |
| Chloe Walker  (10) | 196 |

## St Martin's Junior School, Epsom

| | |
|---|---|
| Rebecca Parker (8) | 196 |
| Jodie Battershell (9) | 197 |
| John Vagg (10) | 197 |
| Allan Macleod (10) | 198 |
| Henry Glasford (9) | 198 |
| Ali Raja (9) | 199 |
| Danielle Carvey (10) | 199 |
| Kieran Rose (10) | 200 |
| Katie Williams (8) | 200 |
| Haissam Adil (10) | 201 |
| Jodie Rogers (10) | 201 |
| Farah Faheem (10) | 202 |
| Libby Woolgar (9) | 202 |

## Tatsfield Primary School

| | |
|---|---|
| Anya Mooney (10) | 203 |
| Reuben Aitken-Till (10) | 204 |
| Katie Pratt (9) | 205 |
| Daisy Richardson (9) | 205 |
| Martin Barlow (10) | 206 |
| James Tetzner (10) | 206 |
| Chloe Shimmins (10) | 207 |
| Bethany Nairne (10) | 207 |
| Rachel Dickens (9) | 208 |
| Rhys Woodward (10) | 208 |
| Bridey Clifton (9) | 209 |
| Ben Harris (10) | 209 |
| Jessica Salliss (9) | 210 |
| Scott Mathews (10) | 210 |
| Jay White (10) | 211 |
| Jonathan Layton (10) | 211 |
| Emma Knights (10) | 212 |
| Susannah Layton (10) | 213 |
| Emma Sheehan (9) | 214 |
| Jim Blackman (9) | 215 |
| Helen Gorringe (10) | 216 |
| Emma Louise Pratt (10) | 216 |
| Bradley Waite (11) | 217 |
| Matthew Benison (10) | 217 |
| Esther Richmond (10) | 218 |

Edward Irving  (10)     219
Dominic Menham  (10)     220
Charles Boys  (10)     220
Samuel Minahan  (9)     221
Rosy Kingdon  (10)     221
Ryan Reynolds  (11)     222
Alex Holmes  (10)     222
Joseph Geddes  (9)     223
Ollie Bracey  (10)     223
Elliott Griffiths  (9)     224

**Weyfield Primary School**
Jo Herzig  (8)     224
Emma Cox  (9)     225
Naomi Shotter  (8)     225
Bethany Cox  (9)     225
Gemma Brock  (6)     226
Shelby Dodd  (7)     226
Mahrazul Chowdhury  (7)     226
Shannon Skinner  (8)     227
Missy Chalk  (8)     227
Jessica Chatfield  (8)     227
Anh Nguyen  (8)     228
Jimmy Lemon  (9)     228
Melvin Brown  (8)     228
Rosie Clarke  (8)     229
Jack Orledge  (8)     229
Siân Morley  (8)     229
Finlaye Bartlett  (9)     230
Didier Fung  (9)     230
Samantha Newman  (8)     230
Carla Brenton  (9)     231
Jake Smith  (9)     231
Cameron Davis  (8)     231
Kirsten Rayner  (10)     232
Tekisha Bown  (9)     232
Jack Harvey  (9)     233
Charlotte Lee  (9)     233
Harry Moss  (7)     234
Steven Whitehouse  (7)     234
Daniel Gomme  (7)     234

| | |
|---|---|
| Lucy Bunyan  (7) | 235 |
| Jack Stevens  (9) | 235 |
| Mariah Skinner  (7) | 235 |
| Katie Bookham  (7) | 236 |
| Jordan Wheeler  (7) | 236 |
| Daniel Morter  (7) | 236 |
| James West  (7) | 237 |
| David Green  (9) | 237 |
| Connor Higgs  (9) | 237 |
| Abigail Tidbury  (9) | 238 |
| Ryan Smith  (9) | 238 |
| Rachel Holland  (8) | 238 |
| Thomas Bullen  (9) | 239 |
| Connie Bell  (9) | 239 |
| Charlotte McNamara  (9) | 239 |
| Allison Smith  (9) | 240 |
| Brooke Spinks  (9) | 240 |
| James Taylor  (9) | 241 |
| Ben Harding  (10) | 241 |
| Daniel Bunyan  (9) | 242 |
| Shannon Ingleton  (9) | 242 |
| Ella Purrett  (9) | 243 |
| Nathan Salmon  (10) | 243 |

# The Poems

# The Magic Box

*(Based on 'Magic Box' by Kit Wright)*

I will put in the box . . .
A giant coiling snake
A dragon's sparkling fire
A killer whale with a huge tummy.

I will put in the box . . .
A big rock man
A machine called Relingquisht.

I will put in the box . . .
Some little elves
Some live miniature animals
And a cloud.

My box is made from . . .
The silk of a rainbow
The scales of a dragon
The sparks from a star.

My box will take me to
The Atlantic Ocean
To ride on the waves!

**Martin Dixon  (7)**
**Bishopsgate School**


# The Laugh Poem

If I come face to face
You can call me a disgrace.

I will make you smile
With a crocodile.

My friend gave me an autograph
Which really made me laugh and laugh.

Just to make you laugh
I will run to Bath.

**James Dermott  (7)**
**Bishopsgate School**

# Crazy Poem

I want to buy a book
but I don't have a hook.

I want to be the best
but I don't have a vest.

I want to be good
but I don't have a hood.

I am sad
but I'm not bad.

I think I know how to make you smile
I will go and run a mile.

I think I know how to make you laugh
I'll just go and have a bath.

Now wipe that frown from off your face,
because I really think you're ace.

**Daniel Knox  (7)**
**Bishopsgate School**


# The Magic Box

*(Based on 'Magic Box' by Kit Wright)*

I will put in the box . . .
Some gold rings and necklaces
A magic money tree
A wet piece of a blue whale's tail

I will put in the box . . .
A star that gives you three wishes
A clock that tells you every time in the wide world
A magic horn of a goat

My box is made from . . .
Gold and silver coins
I shall go with my box to a land
Which gives you wishes.

**Matthew Tate  (7)**
**Bishopsgate School**

# The Magic Box

*(Based on 'Magic Box' by Kit Wright)*

I will put in the box . . .
Gold coins and jewels
Red, yellow, blue and green
With hot smiling flames that burn
Intruders.

I will put in the box . . .
Red petals from a tulip
That turns into wings.
Big chocolate castles
With sweets inside it.

My box is made from . . .
Jumping, dancing flames
With smoke that twirls
Around the room.

I shall fly to sunny Florida.

**Tom Capsey (8)**
**Bishopsgate School**


# The Wild Western Flying Pig

The wild western flying pig dives
Like Colossus swooping
Through the jungle leaves,
He soars across the seven seas.

He has claws that chop in half
Those little fleas
Anyone who disobeys him
Shall fall to his knees.

His back is as strong as a wall,
He eats like a pterodactyl.

**Stephen Kahn (8)**
**Bishopsgate School**

# The Magic Box

*(Based on 'Magic Box' by Kit Wright)*

I will put in my box . . .
The sparkly horn from a multicoloured unicorn
The smell of the most colourful rose
A slice of the most fluffiest cloud.

I will put in my box . . .
A little bottle of glittering magic dust
Three violet wishes that come true fast
A pencil that can make things you write come true.

I will put in my box . . .
A piece of a glittery, colourful rainbow
A bit of cat's fur
A magic book of secrets and wishes.

My box is made from ice, gold and jewels
With stars on the lid and secrets in the corners.

I shall fly in my box to an imaginary world
I will play with the butterflies and make
Daisy chains on the clouds.

**Gina Clare (7)**
**Bishopsgate School**


# Fear

Fear is red like blood upon a dying person
It tastes like a mouthful of gumshield putty
It smells like cabbage cooked on a Sunday
It sounds like a scary ghost
It looks like a fierce dragon
It feels like burning fire
It reminds me of a fierce alien.

**Toby Milne-Clark (8)**
**Bishopsgate School**

# The Magic Box

*(Based on 'Magic Box' by Kit Wright)*

I will put in the box . . .
Four-leaved clovers which bring really good luck,
A shiny unicorn's horn and a glittering slice of rainbow.

I will put in the box . . .
A real piece of gold and Queen Victoria's favourite necklace,
A magic star which glows in the dark and
A soft snowflake which will never melt.

I will put in the box . . .
A butterfly's wing which will take you anywhere,
A wonderful coin that you can buy anything with.

My box is made from . . .
Beautiful white feathers and light blue leather
With pink purple and yellow butterflies.

In my box . . .
I shall go to Switzerland and walk to the park near the church,
I shall go to the chocolate factory and on cable cars, going up to
The top of the mountain.

**Zara Hillary (7)**
**Bishopsgate School**


# Fear

Fear is black like a haunted house
It looks like a dark torture room
It reminds me of a black devil
It smells like my brother's socks
It tastes like a raw clove of garlic
It sounds like a firing gun
It feels like the end of the world.

**Billy Bauder (8)**
**Bishopsgate School**

# The Magic Box

*(Based on 'Magic Box' by Kit Wright)*

I will put in the box . . .
A glittery wonderful slice of rainbow
A slimy touch of a tongue
A potion that lets me rule the lands.

I will put in my box . . .
Silver butterfly wings
Silver jewels and rubies
A treasure chest with gold coins.

I will put in my box . . .
A dog's tail with gold spots
A flying tiger to take me anywhere I want and guard me
A spell that will make me fly

My box is made from gold and silver and bronze
I shall fly to far off lands never heard of before and explore!

**Joshua Crew  (7)**
**Bishopsgate School**


# My Baby Brother

My silly brother spills his drink
And food, all around the table.
He throws his toys and screams and yells
As loud as he is able.

My silly brother pulls my hair
And spills all his tea.
He throws his clothes on the floor
And blames it all on me!

**Jasmine Tucker  (9)**
**Bishopsgate School**

# The Magic Box

*(Based on 'Magic Box' by Kit Wright)*

I will put in the box . . .
The bravery of a dinosaur
Grenades that explode violently,
The flap of a butterfly's wing.

I will put in the box . . .
A computer that spells in your head,
Ancient jokes which make you laugh,
The noise of a dog growling.

My box is made from very, very strong steel
With padlocks.
It has four openings with padlocks super-duper strong,
It has fire on the lids.

I shall surf in my box on the tidal waves
From the West Indies to North Korea!

**Mason Rainier-Kirkwood  (7)**
**Bishopsgate School**


# If I Was . . .

If I was a hurricane
I would destroy everything in my way.

If I was the Incredible Hulk
I would kill all the baddies.

If I was an alien
I would fly the galaxy for life.

If I was Superman
I would catch the baddies and put them in jail.

But I am only me, and not Superman,
Or the Incredible Hulk, or an alien,
Or a hurricane, I am just me.

**Alexander Riddiford  (9)**
**Bishopsgate School**

# The Magic Box

*(Based on 'Magic Box' by Kit Wright)*

I will put in the box . . .
A piece of a silky mermaid's tail
A wonder of all wonders
The shiny and colourful fluff of a cloud.

I will put in the box . . .
A piece of a cat's claw
The softest heart of all hearts
The horn from a silvery magic unicorn.

I will put in the box . . .
A blue pencil that never shortens
A shooting star that gives a wish
A butterfly wing that takes me home.

My box is made from the finest blue leather
Decorated with fairy wings and the best pieces of gold.

I shall go to Disneyland to fly on the roller coaster.
Even though my box is small.

**Olivia Grist  (7)**
**Bishopsgate School**


# Hate

Hate is black like a deep hole underground
It looks like a dark shadowy alleyway
It smells like blood on a lion's victim
It tastes like a gulp of hot air going into your mouth
It sounds like a gunshot in the darkness
It reminds me of the war in Iraq
It feels like a gravestone that is cold and old.

**Jamie White  (8)**
**Bishopsgate School**

# The Magic Box
*(Based on 'Magic Box' by Kit Wright)*

I will put in the box . . .
My naughty dog's gold collar,
A see-through spy kit,
A mini, silent, gold fire pistol.

I will put in the box . . .
A funny blue monkey
The smoke of a smelly dragon
A funny long snake with a floppy tail
The touch of a bird's feather.

I will put in the box . . .
A piece of cloud
A dancing crocodile
Some ugly goblins.

My box is made from happy dancing flames
With strange smoke.

I shall fly to the Caribbean.

**Daniel Frogatt (7)**
**Bishopsgate School**


# Hate

Hate is red like a volcano erupting on a cloudy day
It reminds me of an angry cat
It smells like a devil's potion
It tastes like smelly cats' fur all over the house
It sounds like very fierce thunder
It feels like a tree falling down to the ground
It looks like a dark, gloomy dungeon.

**James Cars (8)**
**Bishopsgate School**

# The Magic Box

*(Based on 'Magic Box' by Kit Wright)*

I will put in the box . . .
A slice of glistening rainbow
And a mini rabbit that has wings
Its tail is like a cloud.

I will put in the box . . .
A pointed unicorn's horn which is
Pink, silver and yellow
And an everlasting tree
That grows sweets and a
Butterfly's wing.

My box is made from glass with diamonds
And rubies which sparkle like a shooting star.

I will fly in my box to the best theme park
In the universe.

**Scarlett Irons  (7)**
**Bishopsgate School**


# The Magic Box

*(Based on 'Magic Box' by Kit Wright)*

I will put in the box . . .
A magical bag that is transparent
Inside silvery snowflakes
Which gives me white, bird-like wings to fly.

I will put in the box . . .
Whirling, twisting tornadoes that float
Into space and vanish!
The sound of the sea
The finest stone from Vesuvius.

My box is made from fur
As soft as the softest cloud.

I shall fly taking pictures of the weather
And the pictures come home with me.

**David Cavanagh  (7)**
**Bishopsgate School**

# The Magic Box
*(Based on 'Magic Box' by Kit Wright)*

I will put in the box . . .
Toy animals made from feathers
Magic pens and unicorn's horn
Lots of books.

I will put in the box . . .
A gold star from the sky
A juicy apple pie
Ten big purple wishes
A magic white swan.

I will put in the box . . .
A big disco ball
Music and dancers
Sweets, cookies and cakes
Balloons and pink, yellow,
Purple and blue streamers.

My box has gold scales
Long coloured streamers with cat's fur everywhere
It has stars on the lid
Pick one and make a wish.

My box has . . .
Little maids with long, curly hair
Red hearts that never run out of magic dust.

I shall fly in my box to sweet land and have a party
I shall touch the clouds on the way
Fly over the sea and wave at boats
And live in a house of sweets.

**Isabel Murray  (7)**
**Bishopsgate School**

# The Magic Box

*(Based on 'Magic Box' by Kit Wright)*

I will put in the box . . .
A bit of a horse's tail
The lovely smell of a butterfly's breath
The scales of a rough snake.

I will put in the box . . .
A princess in a dress
A piece of moon that you can still see in sunlight
A pencil that will write when you get tired.

I will put in the box . . .
Lots of gold coins
Rubbers that will rub out for you
Lots of sparkly crowns.

My box is made from silky butterfly wings,
I shall ride on a unicorn to the moon
And be the best moon flyer.

**Nicola Penn  (7)**
**Bishopsgate School**


# The Hamster

Harry the hamster has teeth like bulbs,
And ears like those of little moles.

He's as small as a real live bat,
And his hair sticks up like a terrified cat.

He's as brown as mud and snores like thunder,
With a little thud he goes off to wander.

His tummy is itchy, he scratches it a lot,
His nose you'd call a tiny pink dot.

His spine is long, just like his tail,
And in a race, he just won't fail!

**Jonathan Davies  (8)**
**Bishopsgate School**

# The Magic Box
*(Based on 'Magic Box' by Kit Wright)*

I will put in the box . . .
A giant peach all round and sparkly
The finest silk a silkworm could make
And an Egyptian mummy.

I will put in the box . . .
The best chocolate in the world
And Queen Victoria's best piece of jewellery.

I will put in the box . . .
A singing crocodile
A piece of the sun
And an everlasting slice of rainbow.

My box is made from . . .
The softest velvet in the world for its lid
Hinges made from starlight
The corners made from bits of the universe.

I shall go in my box to the end of the world,
Fall off a cliff which leads into space and
Become an astronaut and go to Mars.

**Omar Ahmed (7)**
**Bishopsgate School**


# Sadness

Sadness is black like the wings of the wisest bird
It feels like a pain in your eyes
It reminds me of the two World Wars
It tastes like the water drop of an eye
It smells like the salt of the sea
It sounds like a dolphin calling for its mother
It looks like a person swimming in the salty sea.

**Alexander Fallegger (7)**
**Bishopsgate School**

# The Magic Box
*(Based on 'Magic Box' by Kit Wright)*

I will put in my box . . .
A magic tree made of snow and glitter
A pencil that lets you write anything.

I will put in my box . . .
A golden treasure
A rabbit that talks
A tiger that flies in the air.

I will put in my box . . .
A piece of glittery star
A fiery dragon that's black
Three wishes that are cool
A lion that talks strangely.

My box is made from . . .
Ice that is very golden
Rough dinosaur skins that are green
With stars on the lid.

I shall go to Never Never Land
Jump on all the clouds.
And snorkel in the Indian Ocean.

**Riccardo Leoni-Sceti (7)**
**Bishopsgate School**


# Love

Love is red like floating across white fluffy clouds
On a sunny day
It tastes like beautiful raspberries and cream
It sounds like a fairy singing romantically
It feels like you're having the best time ever
It looks like a beautiful butterfly in a patch of flowers
It reminds me of dolphins calling to me
It smells like sweet perfume going up your nose.

**Eva Gripenstedt (8)**
**Bishopsgate School**

# Robbie The Rabbit

Robbie the rabbit has pointed ears like spikes
He digs and burrows underground pipes

Although you think he's a kind one
He can go as fast as an F1

He can't camouflage as well as a snake
But what he can do is eat a big cake

He gets into a very big rage
If there is a terrific ice age

He can smell the sense of danger
But he doesn't know where to find a manger

He has not seen a wild fox
But he can hide in a big box

He can probably jump a bale
But he barely ever wails

He has never seen electric plugs
But he can take really big glugs

He can eat a lot of grass
But he never goes to class

He has been to a lot of places
But he has had to get out of many chases.

**Henry Milton  (8)**
**Bishopsgate School**

# Hunger

Hunger is dark grey like the storm in New London
It looks like a flat ball lying on the floor
Hunger feels like the feather of the last dying bird
It reminds me of dying of starvation
It tastes like burnt cigarettes on a burnt floor
It smells like volcanoes erupting one by one
Hunger sounds like an earthquake rumbling.

**Michael Fallegger  (7)**
**Bishopsgate School**

# Spotty The Springbok

Mr Springbok who are you, are you cold?
Are you lonely, or are you old?

Mr Springbok, are you fast?
Will he ever talk at last?

Mr Springbok, where's your pack?
Did they put you under attack?

Mr Springbok, can you camouflage
Or will you stand out large?

Mr Springbok, are you cute
Or will you cause a dispute?

Mr Springbok do you eat passers-by
Or will you say hi or bye?

Mr Springbok are you gold?
Is that what you're told?

Mr Springbok do you eat fish?
Shall we have a dish?

Mr Springbok, are you dangerous?
Shall I go before you get ferocious?

**David De Villiers  (8)**
**Bishopsgate School**


# Anger

Anger is red like a volcano erupting
It feels like me dying
It looks like a devil staring straight at me
It reminds me of when my father breaks friends with my mother
It smells like a fierce fire getting closer
It tastes like poison in me
It sounds like my mother screaming.

**Alex Pagnoni  (8)**
**Bishopsgate School**

# Through My Window

I looked through my window on a cold winter's night
I can see the flickering of the monstrous moon
Shadows are like ghosts dancing on the ground
Birds fighting for worms and twigs at noon.

Through my window on a cold winter's night
I can see the sway of sharp blades of grass
Blowing gently to the rhythm of the icy wind
Icicles are hanging from branches as cold as brass.

Through my window on a cold winter's night
I see silver flakes fall to a layer of white snow
The trees in the night groan like ghosts
The foxes fight, not friends but foe.

Through my window on a cold winter's night
I hear the wind blow through the trees
I see the birds fly past my window,
It is a freezing, cold, biting breeze.

**Elizabeth Dunning  (9)**
**Bishopsgate School**


# Happiness

Happiness is multicoloured like a rainbow on a sunny day
It smells like flowers, chocolate and sweets
It tastes like melting sweets, running through your mouth
It sounds like a disco party coming from a nearby village
Happiness feels like snow falling on heads
Happiness looks like a pop star dancing
It reminds me of my mum and dad's wedding on a great island.

**Sandra Isautier  (8)**
**Bishopsgate School**

# Marrow The Eagle

Marrow the eagle soars swiftly through the air
Protecting its nest like a lion guarding its lair.

It is the god of the jungle and has such powers
After a hard day's hunting, he goes by the waterfall
for a cooling shower.

He can hear a drip of water falling on a leaf, a thousand miles away
He can sense a hopeless baby chick that's in danger,
it will not escape its prey.

Marrow the eagle is like the night's pitch-black sky
Like a blackness you see when you close your eyes
before you cry.

Up close you see his talons as sharp as a spear
Mice panic and run for cover with uncontrollable fear.

His dark blue amazing eyes hunt for tiny creatures in open land
He finds killing his prey rather viciously grand.

**Zachery Donohoe  (8)**
**Bishopsgate School**


# Tiger In The Jungle

To the tiger, the jungle is a loving brother,
His home there is like no other.

Camouflaged with orange and black like a bumblebee,
But sadly, how endangered can one be?

The tiger puts us in danger, as a meat eater.
Face to face you would not want to meet her.

One sudden movement could draw her attention.
From a doze in a shady dream . . . please do not mention.

Tiger, tiger do you have any enemies?
Yes, of course - but I hide in the trees.

When on safari, I would like to see you,
But from the safety of the truck, what a lovely view!

**Jacob Belcher  (9)**
**Bishopsgate School**

# Tanner The Tiger

Tanner the tiger's fur is as orange as ember
He's the jungle's greatest member

His tail whips about like a plane going from side to side
When he sees his prey he opens his mouth very wide

Tanner's teeth are as glistening and as white as snow
When he smiles they're in a nice neat row

He bares his fangs and lets out a ghost-like growl
A sound that spooks a hooting owl

In sleep he closes the curtains on his big black eyes
And purrs like a kitten less than half his size

When he wakes he stretches like an elastic band
And begins to hunt on the entire land

His claws are as sharp as a dagger's blade
He eats his prey under a tree in the shade.

**Parker Walls  (8)**
Bishopsgate School


# Bobby The Bunny

Bobby the bunny has ears as smooth as silk
His fur is as white as milk.

He has legs as bouncy as a pogo stick
He bounces over the fence for a trick.

Bobby is white, camouflaged in snow
His favourite food is carrots you know.

Bobby the bunny has blue eyes
He jumps around in search of pies.

Bobby the bunny is so thin
So he can jump through a ring of bins.

Little baby Bobby goes to sleep
Then does a very quick beep.

**Natasha Scott  (8)**
Bishopsgate School

# Double Trouble

My brother calls me Stinky Socks,
I call him Goldilocks
He calls me Fat Face
I call him Nut Case.

Then my mum comes in and calls us Double Trouble!

My brother throws his clothes on the ground
I put mine elsewhere.
He throws his toys around,
He makes me pick them up, it's not fair!

Then my mum comes in and calls us Double Trouble!

My brother goes to bed at eleven
I go at seven.
He gets up at five to nine,
I'm always up on time.

But my mum still comes in and calls us Double Trouble!

But now he's gone, gone to live alone
I will miss him a lot -
We had so much fun
Fighting at home.

**Alyssa Heritier  (9)**
**Bishopsgate School**


# Hate

Hate is red like the blood of death
Hate tastes like cow's liver
Hate smells like dead corpses
Hate sounds like the Devil laughing
Hate looks like the Devil at his happiest
Hate feels like the guts of a cow
Hate reminds me of people screaming.

**Jackson Smith  (8)**
**Bishopsgate School**

# Smarty Pants

My smarty cat
Walks me home from school
He walks so posh
I say he looks like a silly cat drawl.

I usually just run across the road
But every Friday it's his duty
To take care of me
He says, 'Meow, meow. *No!*'
It gets so boring because we
Look left and right and right and left,
Every Friday in a row.

And then at night I'd apologise
And he says, 'Meow, meow, too.'
Then I'd say I'll stroke him till the end of the day,
Then I tug him away.

Every night we cuddle up and he licks me nighty-night,
In the morning, he licks me and I wake with a sigh
Of *happiness!*

**Anuschka Bahlsen  (10)**
Bishopsgate School


# Happiness

Happiness is pink like the depths of our bodies
It smells like sweet smelling roses
It sounds like the beating of a bird's wing
It looks like a banner posted across the door of a party
It feels like paper, pink as a flamingo
It reminds me of Elizabeth Lunn
It tastes like the bark of an old tree.

**Jennifer Cade  (8)**
Bishopsgate School

# Over Mossflower Wood

Over Mossflower Wood I find many magical things
I can hear the little ladybirds sing so sweet.
And the butterfly dancing to their song,
And crickets, they rub their legs to keep up with the beat.

Over the wood I find many magical things,
I can see the glistening lake like shining stars
And the trees swishing to and fro in the breeze,
Look closely and you will see ladybirds eating chocolate bars.

I like to view the evergreen growing on the tree
And every animal is like a shooting star to me.
I like to see the world go by as a snowflake,
Come and have some tea with me and see.

Little pixies love to see dragonflies singing with glee,
I love to see the pixies dance and shout and play.
So every time I look out the Mossflower window,
I can see the world happening this way.

Come and see what I have seen and you'll believe it too,
To the sights I will be a friend forever.
But if you come, you must bring an open mind,
Then we can witness the magical things together.

**Eleanor DiBiase  (9)**
**Bishopsgate School**


# Anger

Anger is red like pouring blood coming from a dying bird
It reminds me of a rhino coming straight at me
It tastes like mouldy carrots boiling in a pan
Anger smells like tyres burning
Anger sounds like nails scratching down a blackboard
It looks like the Devil laughing in Hell
It feels like your hand is on fire and burning to ashes.

**Jamie Abbott  (8)**
**Bishopsgate School**

# From My Window

From my window I can see amazing things for you and me,
I can see the sun's happy smiles, smiling through the day.
I can see tiny ants climbing the large trees,
Like big hands coming to play.

I can see the silver glitter coming from the moon,
I can hear the birds singing nursery rhymes.
I can see little bunnies watching their mum,
I can see butterflies humming to their tune.

Fantastic things from my window I can see
The rabbits are munching on golden carrots.
Foxes attack each other in the dark green forest,
Snakes are fighting with the coloured beautiful parrots.

From my window I can see a deer sprinting as fast as lightning,
I can see the frogs leaping over the pond.
In my pond I can see flying fish jumping over my reflection.
I can see the snakes slithering and sliding beyond.

Look out of my window and you will see
The opportunities I've had to view and enjoy.
All you need is a key to your imagination
It will feel like you have the most amazing toy.

**Nadia Raslan  (9)**
Bishopsgate School


# Snow

Snowboard sliding silently
Through the smooth snow.
The slush slips slyly through,
The snowflakes tumbling
To the soft surface.
Twinkle through the sky,
Sparkly snow shining in the sunlight.

**Alexander Pearson  (10)**
Bishopsgate School

# In My Bag

In my bag there's an entire new world,
My books are trapped like convicts.
My pencils are curling and hurling pearls,
The king of sharpenings has a knave.

My ruler is the king of all times in my bag,
His royal knave has a flag.
On the flag there is a tag,
It's all in my bag.

My rubber is blubbery,
My pencil case is bubbly,
My pen is slippery,
It's all in my bag.

In my bag there's lots of dust,
In my bag there's a whole new world.
Sometimes it creates a gust,
In my bag, there's everything.

**Edward Henshaw (9)**
**Bishopsgate School**


# First Day

New rooms, new faces,
New lessons, new places.
A science lab,
Dinner's fab,
Soccer's a treat
New boots on my feet.
A music school
Noise is the rule,
History and Vikings
It's very exciting.
Maybe it's fate
I'm at Bishopsgate.

**James Barlow (9)**
**Bishopsgate School**

# Magic Box

*(Based on 'Magic Box' by Kit Wright)*

I will put in the box . . .
The pink horn of a silky unicorn,
A brown rabbit's fluffy tail.
A small golden tree with all your wishes on,
The scale of a purple snake.

I will put in the box . . .
The two finest silk cloths ever made,
An everlasting strawberry fudge with cream.
An orange tabby cat which turns into a dog.

My box is made from the finest fur of a tiger
And the lid from a zebra.

I shall ride my box through the towns of France,
Then fly to Italy to climb the Leaning Tower of Pisa!

**Sarah Wiggins  (7)**
**Bishopsgate School**


# Hurricane Ivan

I am a hurricane,
Evil and dark.
I hide in the chaos
All alone.
But I do not care
Because I am a hurricane,
And I destroy towns.

I am Ivan,
A hurricane, fierce.
I flood nations
And I pierce
Holes in the roofs
Of houses.

**Elliott Dawson  (9)**
**Bishopsgate School**

# There Is A Monster In My Closet!

There is a monster in my closet,
He has bulging, bulbous eyes,
That thing in my closet is so gigantic,
I fear one day he will touch the skies.

There is a monster in my closet,
He's really very green,
It is so very scary, terribly scary,
He's incredibly wicked and mean.

There is a monster in my closet,
I think in there too he may have a friend,
But I am not sure and too scared to look,
I think he hides round the bend.

There is a monster in my closet,
Now I've seen his friend who's name is Boo.
There is no longer a monster in my closet,
There are two!

**Cooper Robinson  (9)**
**Bishopsgate School**


# If I Dared To Be A Devil

If I dared to be a devil,
Who prowled around the streets at night,
I would fly around by the day
And give people a bit of a fright.

If I had a house I would wreck it down
To tiny little bits,
Then I would eat it and fire would come
From my mouth
And smoke from my nostrils and ears.

I steal from markets to find my food
And barrels of beer to drink.
They think that I am very rude,
(If I tried to swim, I'd sink!)

**Ben Lowe, Henry Parker & Jack Turner  (9)**
**Bishopsgate School**

# The Sea

All different fishes in the sea and the ocean,
The blue liquid looks like potion.
The Black Sea is so salty,
That fish - beauty!

Look at the fish, it is so old,
I like looking at the waves fold.
I would like to go to the Red Sea
That's where I want to waterski.

Look at the view, it's so bright,
I like it with orange light.
Here comes a shark - oh no!
That fish won't swim away - too slow!

Look at the dolphin
She says 'Hi!'
When she dives
She looks like she can fly.

**Julie El-Bacha (9)**
**Bishopsgate School**


# What Would I Be?

If I had warm fur
I would curl up and go to sleep.
If I had a rough tongue
I would lick myself clean.
If I had green eyes
I would be able to spot a tiny ant.
If I had sensitive ears
I would be able to hear a mouse scurry by.
If I had posh paws
I would walk past elegantly and show off.
What would I be?

**Eleanor Heanue (9)**
**Bishopsgate School**

# Inside My Treasure Box

Inside my treasure box
I keep my special rings,
My Spanish doll from Mummy
And my sister's 'borrowed' things.

The box is very tatty,
And also very old.
It once belonged to Great Granny
Or so I have been told.

Where I keep it, is a secret
In a dark and dusty space,
Full of spider's silky cobwebs
That look and feel like lace.

It's getting very full now,
Like a squirrel's nut store.
I shall need to have a tidy up,
If I want to keep much more.

**Katie Bowen  (9)**
**Bishopsgate School**


# Thunderbolt

I am a thunderbolt,
Brave and bold.
I am a storm cloud,
Grey and old.

I am a tornado,
I terrorise towns.
Flood countries,
Demolish cities.

People fly in the sky,
High above the midnight sky.

**Sean Dawson  (9)**
**Bishopsgate School**

# Dreams

When I go to bed
I cuddle up to teddy.
Mummy tucks me in
And then I know I'm ready.
I go to sleep
And many dreams come.

Fairies, frogs,
Ghouls and gogs.
Cats, dogs,
Bats and logs,
Some are good
Some are bad
Some are fun
Some are sad.

I hear the bell -
Time to get up!
Fantasies go
But I know
They're there.
Nobody knows
But we do.

**Charlotte Jarman (9)**
**Bishopsgate School**


# Ziggy

Ziggy, Ziggy, Ziggy who plays the guitar,
And likes going to the Spa.
He can play the drums,
As he hums, hums, hums!
The angels sing
The phone then rings
Ding a ling-a-ling.

**Mia Manduca (7)**
**Bishopsgate School**

# In My Smoky Box
*(Inspired by 'Magic Box' by Kit Wright)*

In my smoky box I would put . . .
The smoke from a hundred dragons, sneezing,
The dust from the old and dreary stars.
The noise from a thousand puppies, pleading.

In my smoky box I would put . . .
The blue cheese from the moon,
Silver glitter from outer space.
The footprint from a cheetah on a sunny afternoon.

In my smoky box I would put . . .
The smelly breath of a hideous troll.
The simmering, sparkling root of all magic,
The first footsteps of a newborn foal.

My box is gold, silver and bronze,
There are stars, moons and suns on my box,
It glitters and sparkles like stars.
Inside, you may find a bright red fox.

I would sail in my box
To a foreign land
Discover new places
And cover beaches with sand.

My box has a golden lock
And a silver key
A yellow thread to hold
My box is secret to me.

It lives in a hole in the floorboards,
Only I look in this space
When I open my box
It's a very secret place.

**Francesca Simcox (9)**
**Bishopsgate School**

# In My Little Sweetie Box

In my little sweetie box are wonderful treasures,
There are red and orange lollipops
Standing like a crowd of people in a street,
I love to eat their brightly coloured tops.

In my little sweetie box are wonderful treasures,
There is a chocolate river flowing by,
Softly and slowly, as smooth as velvet,
I would like to swim in it or put it in a pie.

In my little sweetie box are wonderful treasures,
There are many pink and white marshmallow trees,
That blew me gently their way,
I wonder if they're full of busy bees.

In my little sweetie box are wonderful treasures,
There is a gingerbread house with a Jelly Baby door,
That took my breath away,
It looks delicious, of that I am sure.

In my little sweetie box are wonderful treasures,
There are Wine Gum chairs and tables,
As squidgy as a feathery pillow,
Have one on me, Aunty Mabel!

In my little sweetie box are wonderful treasures,
There is candyfloss smoke coming out of the chimney,
That makes my heart sing.
I watch it blowing free.

**Annabel Selley  (9)**
**Bishopsgate School**

# In My Secret School Bag

When I open my school bag, I would find . . .
A leaking ink cartridge like a blue river
There would be goldfish swimming around
Making their tiny muscles wiggle and slither

When I open my school bag, I would find . . .
A wishbone as hard as clay
I would wish for a horse to ride
And I'd jump, canter and gallop all day

When I open my school bag, I would find . . .
The sparkling roots from a shooting star
They would shine very yellow and gold
Like the moon shining from afar

When I open my school bag, I would find . . .
A group of dreams from when I was young
I would jump around like a kangaroo
I would have lots of fabulous fun

When I open my school bag, I would find . . .
A broken pencil shattered like blades of grass
Sharpenings would get stuck in my fingers
I would scratch and pick until they last

When I open my school bag, I would find . . .
One million coins of silver and gold
I would spend them on an apple tree
I would collect and eat all the apples I could hold.

**Tara Jameson (9)**
**Bishopsgate School**

# In My Wishing Box

In my wishing box I would put
The shiniest penny from Rome
I would add a sprinkle of dust from the sun
Mixed with some from the man on the moon's home.

I would keep my wishing box . . .
On ice with golden wrapping to keep it proud
In the jungle with ferocious lions guarding it
I'd keep it all wrapped up, safe in a shroud.

I would make it look like . . .
A silver diamond, glittering with all its might
Hidden in a flower box, as its disguise
In the garden of a mountain home, dangling
Like an icicle from a certain height.

The inside would have looked like . . .
A music box for a ballet dancer, singing loudly
Pearls decorated here and there, around the edge
Ballerina's dancing and jumping proudly.

Inside my wishing box I would keep . . .
A thin scary, long droplet of dragon's blood
All magic for eternity and more
A potion bottle holding enough to make a flood.

Inside my wishing box you will find . . .
A collection of mirrors like a funfair
Bright yellow and orange feathers like a bird's
I'd sew these to the clothes I wear.

In my wishing box I would keep . . .
A piece of paper which brings good luck
A charm bracelet that looks like a flower
And a violin, the final note to pluck.

**Aimee Huntington  (9)**
**Bishopsgate School**

# In My Dreams Of Mystery And Wonder

In my dream there's a whole new world
The glimmer of the sun
Sparkles down as elegant as a magical snowflake falling
There are beautiful unicorns that are having fun.

In my vision, there are lots of things
Like two pairs of snow dove wings
And in my dream there are whole moons
And a bird that is coming soon.

In my fantasy and beyond
There are magical things, like you may find in James Bond
There are magical flower petals
Shooting stars that are made of shiny metal.

Down and down and deep, deep in
There is a huge pixie pen
There is magic dust that grants your every wish
An enchanted sea filled with schools of fish.

Swirling and swinging, there is a cocoon
Three shooting stars appear from the moon
Magic that lies amongst the green ground
There are two mysterious eyes on top of a frown

In my mysterious dream
A dripping red lion that pops out and gleams
In my dream, there are icicles which sparkle
And then appeared a mysterious lion tamer, on a bicycle!

The sun is rising, I stretch and wake up
So now my dream is finished and gone
Everything is light and bright, I see the day
It's very tiring, waking up today.

**Grayson Barringer  (9)**
**Bishopsgate School**

# In My Goblet Of Fantasy

Swirling around in my goblet of fantasy
Lies something incredibly secret,
the delicate teardrops from Heaven
sparkle like diamonds on a beautiful bracelet.

Spinning around like a colossal tornado
lies a vicious blood-red viper,
prepared to spring out at any second,
just before the break of dawn as the Earth becomes lighter.

Shimmering like the first star of the summer solstice
is Odysseus venturing back with the Vikings,
who is lost and fearful, miles from home.
The North Sea was most definitely to his liking.

Swishing about like a hustle of people
are the immense crowds of the Chinese new year.
The red Chinese fire-breathing dragon
looked so beastly, the crowd shrank away,
with pounding hearts of fear.

**Lauren Childs  (9)**
**Bishopsgate School**


# Fantasy

Fantasy is light blue
Like the daytime sky.

Fantasy is fun,
It reminds me of a roller coaster.

It smells like a bag of salt,
It tastes like cotton candy.

It looks like Thorpe Park
It sounds like screaming.

Fantasy feels
Like a gushing waterfall.

**George Pearce  (8)**
**Bishopsgate School**

# Magic Box

*(Based on 'Magic Box' by Kit Wright)*

I will put in my box . . .
An everlasting mint chocolate ice cream,
A bag of wish powder
And a token to the most peaceful dream
Ever dreamt.

I will put in my box . . .
A long, sharp, shiny unicorn's horn,
The sound of a wolf crying,
The bravery of Hercules,
A clash of lightning and a soft snowflake.

I will put in my box . . .
A dancing rainbow shining across the sky,
Three golden wishes spoken in Brazilian,
A pond of melted chocolate.

My box is made from peacock feathers,
And petals of the yellowest daffodil,
Its hinges are made of bright, shiny crystals.

I shall fly in my box over the tallest tips of trees,
And land on an island all of my own,
So peaceful and quiet!

**Sam Clarke  (7)**
**Bishopsgate School**

# What Is It?

I found this thing in the jungle
It's really, really small
I have no idea what it is
I thought maybe I'd put it in the hall.

Maybe it's a gun that is a dangerous lion
Or maybe a dragon breathing no fire
Or a human that has ears like an alien
Not it's a seed that keeps on growing higher.

It could be a seed, bigger than an egg
Maybe it's a ghost going to scare everybody away
Or it's a shrunken human as small as a bug
No it's a sea monster that's run a long, long way.

Or maybe it's an alien that has ears like a person
Maybe it's a six-legged war lord
It could be a devil taking everybody to Hell
Oh no! It's a piece of a sword.

It's sharp and pointed
It's as dull as lead
It's as small as a bug
And so I put it in the shed.

**Max Penn  (9)**
**Bishopsgate School**

# Through My Window

What is that outside my window which makes me shiver and scream?
It has the claws of an eagle
And the arms reach out to grab you
How fearful is the root of evil.

Before I go to bed I pray,
'Oh please Lord, can this be my day?'
I hide under my duvet but that's not enough,
Somehow I've got a feeling I'll pay!

Maybe I should cry out or get some help
Or run and leave the room right now.
I feel frozen like an icicle to my bed
By that dreadful, terrifying, shadowy bough.

Am I dreaming or could this be real?
Is it dark still? Bring me sunlight!
Only morning will tell if my fears are true
Of this horrible, monstrous night.

It's morning! A sigh of relief.
The world awakes and birds sing
But I shiver and already I wonder
What the next night will bring!

**Daniel Murray  (9)**
**Bishopsgate School**


# Sadness

Sadness is red like the blood of someone dying in war
It sounds like someone shouting
It feels like your head has been cracked open
It looks like a person with no head
It reminds me of my statue with no head
It smells like rotten food
It tastes like stale water.

**Oliver Goodley  (9)**
**Bishopsgate School**

# In My Box Of Whispers

In my secret chest I have a box of whispers,
Inside there are many secret things,
Angels singing their songs of harmony,
And gently flapping their graceful wings.

In my box of whispers
I can hear a fish's fin,
Flipping and flapping and twisting around
Beneath its scaly skin.

In my box of whispers,
I can hear a baby's cry.
'Hush, hush!' I said to baby
When I had to say goodbye.

I love my box of whispers,
But you must promise not to tell.
That all my things are real and true
And they are really not a spell.

Oh my box of whispers,
I love to hear you call,
But when it's night, I put you away,
To let you dance at your secret ball.

**Claudia Lee  (9)**
**Bishopsgate School**


# Sunflowers

Sunflowers, sunflowers
are so bright.
Sunflowers, sunflowers
glow in the night.
Sunflowers, sunflowers
up so high.
Sunflowers, sunflowers
waiting to be found.

**Rebecca Burgess  (8)**
**Cardinal Newman RC Primary School**

# The Sunflower

Sunflower, sunflower,
you are
so pretty,
you shine
so brightly
in the
sunshine.
Just like a seed
in a
hot pan,
you stand
up so
tall in
the sky.
In the
rain you're
down to the floor.
I love you sunflower.

**Lauren Philp  (8)**
Cardinal Newman RC Primary School

# Dragonflies

Dragonflies, dragonflies,
Down so low,
Flying in the moon day, all so low.
Flying gently to and fro,
Flying so high in the sky.
Dragonflies, dragonflies,
On the ground,
Staying there waiting to be found.
Why do you stay so shy?

**Gisella Cicero  (8)**
Cardinal Newman RC Primary School

# Sunflower, Sunflower

Sunflower, sunflower,
your lovely petals look
so beautiful in the dazzling sun.

Sunflower, sunflower,
you are so pretty.
As the sun sets and the moon rises,
you look amazing.

Sunflower, sunflower,
you are so bright,
you sparkle in the moonlight.

Sunflower, sunflower,
you look like little suns.

**Tom Fox (8)**
**Cardinal Newman RC Primary School**


# Sunflowers Everywhere

Sunflowers, sunflowers,
How lovely you are,
Your petals are beautiful.

Your stalk is green
With a few leaves on top.

Sunflowers everywhere
Only in spring and summer.

Sunflowers, sunflowers,
Your colours are bright and beautiful,
You have lovely pollen for bees.

**Connor McWalsh (8)**
**Cardinal Newman RC Primary School**

# Sunflowers

Sunflowers, sunflowers how lovely you look
And you have lovely petals.

Sunflowers, sunflowers how colourful you are
And how lovely you grow.

Sunflowers, sunflowers you are so lovely
And you are so lovely to grow.

Sunflowers, sunflowers you stare at me
And you look divine.

Sunflowers, sunflowers you are so beautiful
And you have a lovely green stalk.

Sunflowers, sunflowers you are the best
And I think you look very beautiful.

Sunflowers, sunflowers . . .
I love you.

**Sophie Hosie (8)**
**Cardinal Newman RC Primary School**


# Sunflower

Sunflower, sunflower, you are pretty in the light,
But you are more pretty at night.
Sunflower, sunflower, even when the day is dull,
I look at you and you make me smile.
Sunflower, sunflower, your petals are falling each day I look.
Sunflower, sunflower, I'm getting sadder and sadder
As the days go by.
Is it time for you to go?
Should I say goodbye?

**Carissa Ponan (8)**
**Cardinal Newman RC Primary School**

# My Sunny Sunflowers

My sunflowers are very, very bright,
They are such a beautiful sight.

When I see them standing in a pot,
They start to make me feel very hot.

When I watered them they were very, very tall,
But when I didn't they turned very, very small.

When they were small I felt very, very sad
And I started to turn very, very mad.

So then the next day I went to the shop
And there I found some sunflowers standing in a pot!

So there were my sunflowers standing very tall
And I always watered them so they never got small.

**Sophie Denmead (8)**
**Cardinal Newman RC Primary School**


# Sunflowers

Sunflower, sunflower you're a beautiful yellow colour,
It shines in the sun,
Even in bad weather.

Sunflower, sunflower your colours are so bright.
Sunflower, sunflower I love your bright colours,
Do they have you in garden centres?

Sunflower, sunflower it's time for me to go,
Please can I buy you for my sunflower show?

**Amy Mooney (9)**
**Cardinal Newman RC Primary School**

# Sunflowers

There are three sunflowers,
All of them in a sunny spot,
All of them in a brown pot.
Yellow beams,
That lighten the streams.
The emerald stalks,
The bright turquoise leaves,
All fit into one big brown pot,
In a sunny spot.
Being watered every day,
What a game to play.
But when the winter comes to stay,
Their wake up call is on a summer's day.
    I love sunflowers.

**Susanna Kilburn  (8)**
Cardinal Newman RC Primary School


# Dragon

Children scarer,
Non carer,
Fire breather,
Crocodile teaser,
Pool dipper,
Blood sipper,
Dark night,
Fire bright,
Green skin,
Sly grin,
Dragon.

**Kate Allbrook  (8)**
Cardinal Newman RC Primary School

# Dragon Traitor

Breath breather,
Smell sneezer,
Child snatcher,
Cold matcher,
Heart breaker,
Lamb staker,
Pool dipper,
Blood sipper,
Scratch taker,
Blood maker,
Steak taker,
Night waker,
Green skin,
Sly grin,
*Dragon*.

**Harriet Mulcahy (8)**
**Cardinal Newman RC Primary School**


# Dragon

Fire breather
Man eater
Killing machine
Dark theme
Joy hater
Bone breaker
Sick muncher
Clever hunter
Strong fighter
Good flyer
Sharp claws
Terrible jaws
*Dragon*.

**James Pompei (8)**
**Cardinal Newman RC Primary School**

# Beautiful Sunflower

Sunflower, big and bright,
       shine in the night.

Sunflower, green and yellow,
       will make you play the cello.

Sunflower, big and bold
       will not be cold.

Sunflower, in a pot,
       you're not forgot.

Sunflower, when you die,
       I'll sit and cry.

Sunflower, your wonderful scent,
       is not like cement.

Sunflower, the summertime is fine,
       when you start to shine.
          Sunflower!

**James West  (9)**
**Cardinal Newman RC Primary School**


# Dragon

Dark night,
Fire bright,
Gloomy smoke as he spoke,
Red eyes as he sighs.
Blood dribbles on you
As he nibbles through you.
Heart breaker,
Skeleton maker,
Go and see him if you dare,
But *beware,* he will scare!

**Jodie Horne  (8)**
**Cardinal Newman RC Primary School**

# The Dragon

The dragon sat in his cave
Suntanning in the heatwave.

The dragon sat still
While writing with a quill.

The dragon saw a wizard
Who was causing a blizzard.

The dragon said, 'Can you stop that please,
Because I don't like the cold breeze?'

The dragon said, 'I'll breathe fire on you.'
The wizard replied, 'I wouldn't stop even if I had to eat dew.'

So the dragon breathed fire on the wizard
And there was no more blizzard.

**Fabio Baptista (8)**
**Cardinal Newman RC Primary School**


# The Castle Of Dreaming

When you take a quick look
It makes you shiver all over the spot.
The horrible feeling
Of the castle of dreaming
Is just a horrible feeling to have.

When you take a quick glance
It makes you shiver and dance.
The horrible feeling
Of the castle of dreaming
Is just a horrible feeling to have.

**Claire Côté (8)**
**Cardinal Newman RC Primary School**

# Nasty Dragons

Fierce defender,
Fire breather,
Building ruiner,
Brilliant flier,
Animal slayer,
Evil fighter,
Mean killer,
Human stealer,
Far traveller.

**Alex Dalrymple  (8)**
**Cardinal Newman RC Primary School**


# The Sunflowers

The sunflowers so lovely and bright,
You look at them and feel the light.
The sunflowers they grow so tall,
I think to myself, *I wonder if they'll fall.*
Sunflower, sunflower, please don't die away,
Because if you do I'll cry all day.

**Emily Perryment  (8)**
**Cardinal Newman RC Primary School**


# Emotions

Anger is red like a heart exploding.
Hate is black like a stormy day.
Fear is white like a ghost walking at night.
Sadness is pink like a girl crying.
Happiness is orange like a very hot day.
Love is like two hearts pumping.

**Karl Collins  (10)**
**Cranmer Primary School**

# Colourful Emotions

Anger is red and black
like an amazingly, uncontrollable fire.
Fear is grey and black like a dark,
small cave in a haunted forest.
Happiness is yellow like a bright,
beautiful sunflower.
Hate is dark purple and navy blue
like a spiteful word said to you
in your favourite place by a
close friend or loved one.
Love is red like a loving heart
and a pretty rose on Valentine's Day.
Sadness is green like each blade of grass
which holds your saddest memories.

**Jasmin Salik (10)**
Cranmer Primary School


# Emotions

Anger is red like a red kettle
Exploding with steam.

Fear is pale white like a flower
Always moving.

Happiness is yellow
Like a bright yellow flower.

Sadness is grey like a girl
With tears dripping from her eyes.

Hate is black for no mercy.

Love is pink like a pink heart beating
When somebody finds true love.

**Haroon Nigar (10)**
Cranmer Primary School

# Emotions

Anger is red like the scorching sun.
Hate is purple like a big fat, delicious plum.
Fear is black like the dark spooky sky.
Sadness is blue like tears trickling down my cheeks.
Love is red like the heart thumping hard against the chest.
Happiness is green like the grass growing in spring.
Fun is red like the bright rosy lips.

**Shobana Srikumar (11)**
Cranmer Primary School


# Emotions

Anger is scarlet red like blood rushing through your arteries.
Fear is white like snow in a blizzard.
Happiness is multicoloured like balls in a ball pit.
Hate is pitch-black like a cave in a dark, gloomy forest.
Love is like a pink heart on a card.
Sadness is blue like tears on a person's face.

**Daniel Lyndon (10)**
Cranmer Primary School


# Feelings

Anger is like a red fire burning.
Hate is like a green, grassy field.
Fear is black like outer space.
Sadness is yellow like a yellow scorching sun.
Happiness is blue like the sky.
Love is purple like a marriage ring.

**Zaq Wehilye (10)**
Cranmer Primary School

# Emotions

Anger is red like a mountain erupting.
Hate is black like a group fighting.
Fear is purple like a wild animal chasing you.
Sadness is blue like being left out.
Happiness is orange like winning the lottery.
Love is pink like a primrose.
Laughter is yellow like being happy at every joke said.
Fun is green like having all the attention.

**Michael Ban (10)**
Cranmer Primary School

# Emotions

Anger is red like blood exploding out of your scab.
Hate is orange like a left out orange fruit.
Fear is black like a baby crying because he is scared of the dark.
Sadness is like a lonely shark in the dark.
Happiness is like a birthday party in a big hall.
Love is a boy and girl kissing under a big heart.

**Josh Galloway (10)**
Cranmer Primary School

# Emotion

Fire is red like a house on fire.
Fear is black like someone in the dark.
Happiness is green like grass.
Sadness is white like in a funeral.
Hate is red like blood oozing out of veins, argh!

**Hemesh Patel (10)**
Cranmer Primary School

# A Lake Of Emotions

Anger is red like a long, boiling river of lava
and a devil lurking into the mist.

Hate is as black as the terrible war
with dying people and sharp swords.

Fear is white like a blank, scared, tumult . . . tumultuous
mind with a demon hindering it.

Sadness is blue like a puddle of water
and raindrops falling with anger and hatred.

Happiness is green as new trees and lovely nature,
a shining new leaf which is about to be turned over.

Love is pink as a rose with big, bright petals shimmering
in the light and presence of the sunset.

Fun is purple like winning a football match
and a burning flame saying, 'You can do it!'

**Reecha Patel (10)**
Cranmer Primary School


# Emotions

Anger is red like an exploding fire.
Hate is grey like a swirling whirlpool.
Fear is green like a snapping alligator.
Sadness is blue like a pool of tears.
Happiness is yellow like the sun shining.
Love is red like a shining red rose.
Laughter is orange like a laughing jukebox.
Fun is yellow like a bright sunny day.

**Emma Black (10)**
Cranmer Primary School

# Emotions

*Red* - Anger is red like exploding blood
bursting out of a scab.

*Green* - Hate is green like a plate
of disgusting celery.

*Purple* - Fear is purple like a
hairy cockroach.

*Grey* - Sadness is grey like a cloud
shooting out rain.

*Yellow* - Happiness is yellow like a
bright smiley face.

*Pink* - Love is pink like the brightness
of a rose.

**Samuel Olutola  (10)**
**Cranmer Primary School**


# Emotions

Anger is red like a spurt of fire,
A bull sees red and he runs like mad.

Fear is black like when you see nothing
But you know something's there.

Happiness is yellow, bubbly and joyful
Like a bird's song as it graces the air.

Hate is black, also dark and gloomy,
Once put down it cannot be rubbed out.

Love is pink, bright and contagious,
Once it's caught you, you can't get rid of it.

**Richard Oyin-Adeniji  (11)**
**Cranmer Primary School**

# Emotions

Anger is red like blood dripping out of someone's nose
and making a puddle of blood.
Fear is blue like a tap dripping
and someone coming for you.
Happiness is orange like someone sucking
the juice out of an orange.
Sadness is purple like when you blow your nose
in a handkerchief.
Hate is white like when you breathe on a cold day.
Love is pink like when a girl kisses you and you blush.

**George Moore  (10)**
Cranmer Primary School


# Emotions

Anger is red like blood that is silently dripping.
Fear is purple like when your face turns purple with fear.
Happiness is blue for when the sky is blue, I am happy.
Sadness is grey for when the sky is grey, I am sad.
Hate is black for when you hate, your heart turns black.
Love is white and pink, white like you are floating on a cloud
that is smooth and fluffy and pink is like a soft, cushioned heart
that is full of love.

**Imana Dione  (10)**
Cranmer Primary School


# Emotions

Anger is red like a blazing hot fire.
Fear is white like a pale face.
Happiness is green like a lush meadow.
Hate is gold like lightning smashing down on you.
Love is pink like a solid heart filled with lots of love.

**Lily Jane Richards  (10)**
Cranmer Primary School

# Anger Is . . .

Anger is red like a bonfire,
Hate is black like a deserted dark sky.
Fear is like being high up in the sky
And being able to see the sun clearly.
Sadness is blue like hearing news that someone
has just left you and your eyes are pouring with tears.
Happiness is orange like watching an elephant bath in mud.
Love is pink like a long colourful rainbow.
Laughter is green like a field of bright green grass.

**Sabrina-Maria Anderson (10)**
Cranmer Primary School

# My Emotion Poem

Anger is red like an erupting fire.
Fear is ripe brown like a shiny conker.
Happiness is yellow like the dazzling sun.
Sadness is grey like a rainy day.
Hate is black like mysterious space.
Love is pink like a pink velvet rose.

**Timothy Sintim-Aboagye (10)**
Cranmer Primary School

# S Is For . . .

Slimy, slithering, slow Steve.
He's the slowest rattlesnake on Earth,
but he's sure the most venomous snake on Earth.
When he rattles it's a sign for you to move away,
before you meet your doom.
It could poison you to death so run away!

**Jaimin Sadiwala (9)**
Cranmer Primary School

# B Is For . . .

A ball bounces around and around,
High and low, side to side.
People can kick the ball and throw,
You can play with a ball and play sports,
A ball can do everything.
The ball can be all different colours from the rainbow
And it is big like the sun and they are smooth.
It can roll about, it can play in all weathers
Like rain, sun and all the others.
It can play in all of that.

**Riccardo Ribaudo (9)**
Cranmer Primary School


# M Is For . . .

A moon appears on a dark, damp, spooky night,
But be careful it might give you a fright.
When the moon is born the frights lift up
Ghosts, ghouls, trolls and many more.
Its full of mysteries
That we may never know.
When the sun rises and the moon is beaten,
It will move somewhere else to give a fright back.
When the sun has done his work the moon comes back!

**Isabel Santos (9)**
Cranmer Primary School


# S Is For . . .

A slimy snail runs but hardly can in the hot sun
And stops to take a breath.
Slime is left behind as it moves along.

**Reeya Patel (9)**
Cranmer Primary School

# S Is For . . .

Slithering
Sneakily like a spy,
The poisonous anaconda has a deadly bite.
Life-threatening venom.
Steve is the most venomous in the Galaxy.
Killing king cobras is Steve the spy's special, special job.
Do you want to meet this snake?
Because I don't.

**Vinny Smith (9)**
Cranmer Primary School


# A Is For . . .

A green juicy apple sitting there as fine as can be,
It waits there bored, sour and green,
He's mean, he is very mean,
Have you ever seen the sour and green apple?
The caterpillar comes over, took a bite with big teeth.
It said, 'Don't eat me, I'll go mean.'

**Tyrell Hall (9)**
Cranmer Primary School


# The Wonderful World

The wonderful world has so many things.
I wish the world had no more stings.
All the colours in the sky remind me of the rainbow line.

When I look up at the sky that is so high,
It makes me want to jump and fly.
When I see the sun shine so bright,
I start to look at the beautiful sight.

**Charlotte Gatt (8)**
Cuddington Community Primary School

# Chivvy

Flush the toilet,
Clean your teeth,
Close the door
And phone Mrs Heath.

Tidy your bedroom,
Stop eating sweets,
Open the curtains
And no more treats.

Stop watching TV,
Put away your bike,
You can do the cleaning
And stop copying Mike!

When do I get to do anything I like?

**Jessie Marks  (8)**
**Cuddington Community Primary School**


# The Name Of The Class

Taylor is a sailor,
Nick takes the mick,
Freddie's eating Shreddies,
Lauren is foreign,
Charlie eats barley,
Ellen can be a melon,
Guy makes pie,
Gemma's clever,
Rory likes stories,
Jay likes to play,
Josh thinks he's posh,
Jack has a sack.

**Ellen Gregory-Dade  (9)**
**Cuddington Community Primary School**

# Best Friends

Caring person,
Football player
Party inviter,
Telly watcher,
Football liker,
Goalie saver,
Telling secrets,
Lord of the Rings maniac,
That's what I call a best friend.

**Jay McCloskey  (9)**
**Cuddington Community Primary School**


# Night

Darkness bringer,
Light taker,
Moon giver,
Star holder,
Sun hater,
Black lover,
Day scarer,
Shine stealer.

**Sam Long  (8)**
**Cuddington Community Primary School**


# Snatch

Little runner,
Big adventure,
Three legged,
A little snatcher,
Naughty girl,
Always moans,
Don't tease her . . .

**Alfie Holliday  (9)**
**Cuddington Community Primary School**

# Nature's Soul

Nature's soul is the heart of the forest,
Where the animals roam wildly,
Its beauty is striking, it goes wild growing freely.

The wolves they do howl in the black midnight sky,
The foxes they do hunt prey in the middle of the night,
Then vanish when they spot the dawning light,
And as I walk through the heart of the forest
I feel nature's soul come alive,
And as I feel the morning glory I feel I could fly.

**Megan Dean  (9)**
**Cuddington Community Primary School**


# My Dog Is . . .

My dog is cute, funny, fussy, hyper,
Likes me a lot when I'm eating dinner!
She is fast . . . only on grass,
Eats a lot then she's not so fast.
She's lazy, crazy,
Sometimes she can be naughty,
Sometimes she cannot,
But really I do love her lots and lots and lots.

**Josh Wheeler  (9)**
**Cuddington Community Primary School**


# Autumn Nights

Bonfire's crackling red and white,
Fireworks exploding all through the night,
Trick or treaters knocking at the door,
Adults opening them, handing them treats,
Children's eyes gleaming at these delicious sweets.

**Gemma Hopkins  (9)**
**Cuddington Community Primary School**

# My Guinea Pig

Big guy,
Doesn't like pie.
Fast runner,
Dandelion lover.
He is black and orange and white,
He doesn't like to get into a fight.
He runs away from foxes,
He tries to hide in boxes.
He is my friend
And I can't pretend.
I love him loads
And when I'm older I won't forget him.

**Timothy Bischofer (9)**
**Cuddington Community Primary School**


# Dogs

Dogs, dogs, dogs, dogs, dogs.
Scaring frogs,
Hiding from warthogs.
Sitting on logs,
Frightened by hedgehogs,
Playing in bogs.
Dogs, dogs, dogs, dogs, dogs.

**Hyun Joo Yang (7)**
**Cuddington Community Primary School**


# Arctic Mist

Mist is white like the moon, a polar bear,
The Arctic, which is cold and white.
Mist is silent and creeps across the land
Covering it in a velvet, white blanket.
Its clean smell refreshes the land.

**Thomas Bacon (11)**
**Cuddington Community Primary School**

# Ryan Giggs

Ball chaser,
Left winger,
Left footer.

Free kick taker,
Manchester United player,
Wales player.

Trophy hunter,
Fast runner,
Great player!

**Rhys Crowther (9)**
**Cuddington Community Primary School**


# A Poem About Football

F ootie flicker,
O verhead kick,
O ffside position,
T all goalkeeper,
B oosted ball,
A wesome goal,
L ucky winners,
L ove attacking!

*Manchester United FC.*

**Taylor Wilson (9)**
**Cuddington Community Primary School**


# Mum

Cleans and irons,
Drives a car,
Cooks my food,
Makes my bed,
Buys me things
And most of all she's special!

**Rebecca King (9)**
**Cuddington Community Primary School**

## 10 Things In A Witch's Pocket

A rat's tail,
Trod on snail!
Dogs' fleas,
Rotten peas!
Bats' blood,
Runny mud.
Moulded leg,
Broken peg!
Old people's toes,
A dead rabbit's nose!

**Lauren Stevens (10)**
**Cuddington Community Primary School**


## Golden Goldfish

Flake food eater,
Quick swimmer,
Small creature,
Tail flicker,
Water splasher,
Bubble maker,
Water lover,
Super diver.

**Joseph Stuart (9)**
**Cuddington Community Primary School**


## My Dog Millie

My dog is really quite mad
And is also rather bad.
She's a little scavenger
With a black and white coat,
With coarse short hair.
She's small and loves to bark,
My dog's the best in the world.

**Nick Crego (9)**
**Cuddington Community Primary School**

# Housewife

Cleaner,
Dish washer,
Ironer,
Bill payer,
Meal maker,
Child carer,
Homework helper,
Gardener,
Bed maker,
Pet feeder,
Bird feeder,
Turd cleaner,
Shopper.

**Jonathan Egan  (9)**
**Cuddington Community Primary School**


# My Dog Hamish

My dog is mad
And smells very bad.
He's not very bright
And barks day and night.
He has a wet nose
And sniffs his toes.
He likes to chase cats
And breaks lots of hats.
He's the best dog ever
And I'll love him forever.
*My dog Hamish.*

**Yasmin Al-Khudhairi  (9)**
**Cuddington Community Primary School**

# Dogs

Fast runner,
Big and tougher,
Huge leaper,
Cat chaser,
Hole digger,
Bone burier,
Squirrel chaser,
Ball bouncer,
Frisbie catcher,
Lake paddler.

**Edward Vandyke  (9)**
**Cuddington Community Primary School**


# Nightmares

We all have nightmares,
It really isn't fair.
I always run to my mum
Because it gives me a scare.
It isn't good because I'm tearing out my hair,
Nightmares are really, really not fair.

**Bradley Comfort  (10)**
**Cuddington Community Primary School**


# My Sister

Piano player,
Good shouter,
Very clever,
Boring person,
Short height,
Long talker,
Top moaner.

**Alex Gheorgiu  (9)**
**Cuddington Community Primary School**

# Football

Hat-trick hero,
Three goals to zero.
Cup Final winner,
Fantastic winger.
Free kick taker,
Skilful playmaker.
Tackling defender,
Injury mender.
Attackers scoring,
*The game is not boring!*

**Charlie Bacon (9)**
Cuddington Community Primary School


# The Old Men

There once was a lot of old men
Who used to walk round Big Ben.
When three of them died
The old men started to hide.
Then a year after that,
Now this is a fact
It started all over again.

**Steven Strouvalis (9)**
Cuddington Community Primary School


# Fear

Things we fear
Are never that clear.
It's like an illusion
But it's a total confusion.
Maybe we're scared
Because we're unprepared.

**Thomas Welford (10)**
Cuddington Community Primary School

# The Eagle

Sitting on a mountain high
In the clear sky,
It glares down
To the ground,
Its prey walks into the trap
And suddenly *snap!*
At its speed
It takes a lead
Over any other bird,
The mighty meat eater
Is dangerous to any other
Living thing,
Now it's had its dinner
It flies away
And will come back another day.

**Jordan Pettifer  (10)**
**Cuddington Community Primary School**


# Cat

The cat is black and white,
He always gives me a fright.
In the middle of the night
He pounces for the light.
He likes the moon
Like the fork and the spoon.
He likes the sun,
The sun is like a mum.
A light giving friend
It sends the light around the world
And this is where it ends.

**Matthew Cornish  (11)**
**Cuddington Community Primary School**

# Darkness

Darkness swallows you up into the blinding blackness,
Eats away all traces of joy and happiness.
It is still and quiet, blind like a strange dark veil
Tearing away the light.

You cannot see in the pitch-black gloominess,
Starless skies, blackened by clouds.
Like an eclipse, dull and cheerless.
Darkness brings sadness, spooky, coal-black, sooty.

It is silent, not a sound heard, terrifying,
Sitting in a corner.
No light, not even from the moon,
Inky and illuminated all around.

**Alicia Mirza (10)**
**Cuddington Community Primary School**


# Man U Acrostic

M idfield madness Giggs and Keane,
A ttacking van Nistelrooy trying to play it clean.
N eville, Gary working hard,
C hristano Ronaldo competing against Lampard.
H oward saving shots all round,
E ric Djemba-Djemba falling on the ground.
S erious Rooney swinging in shots,
T oe-punting Forlan laughing lots and lots.
E ager defenders Rio and O'Shea,
R ocking fans, having lots to say.

F erguson applauding the exiting game,
C ome to Man U because all the other teams are lame.

**Sammy Gruet (9)**
**Cuddington Community Primary School**

# In The Shadows

In the shadows dark and gloomy,
Shadows are spooky,
Shadows are here,
Shadows are there,
Shadows are everywhere,
Shadows are terribly dark,
It will be frightening to find my own shadow
Creeping towards me in the dark, gloomy night.

**Samad Mirza (9)**
Cuddington Community Primary School


# My Two Cats

I have two cats
Who like sleeping on people's laps,
Chasing each other around the house,
Catching their prey, it's a mouse.
They run around quick and fast,
Watching them go zooming past.
My cats are the best cats in the world
And no one can ever replace them.

**Daniella Milan (9)**
Cuddington Community Primary School


# Laughter

Laughter is like a warm memory,
It is filled with happiness.
It is like a box of warm popcorn
Next to a warm radiator.
It is infectious laughter,
It is like a bottle of champagne fizzing up.

**Joseph Jordan (10)**
Cuddington Community Primary School

# The Cat

Forever staring,
Never glaring.
Forever glad,
Never sad.
She purrs as she rubs against your leg,
She'll enjoy it so, she's bound to beg.
I remember,
Last December
I found in a box,
The colours of a fox,
A little kitten,
Oh so smitten
Under the Christmas tree
Waiting for me,
To open on Christmas Day!

**Georgina Rowe (10)**
**Cuddington Community Primary School**


# 10 Things In A Witch's Pocket

Black cat,
Crooked hat,
Spotty nose,
Dead rose,
Red blood,
Steamy hut,
Smelly mutt,
Rabbits hopping,
Bubble popping,
Burping cauldron.

**Chloe Hardy (9)**
**Cuddington Community Primary School**

# Christmas Time

Lots of presents from Santa,
Listening to the reindeer while they canter,
Sitting by the fireside,
Wanting to go for a ride,
Santa comes in his sleigh,
No need to pay,
Drinking hot chocolate,
Yum, yum, yum,
A piece of pudding in my tum,
I like Christmas with my family.

**Rhianna Robinson  (9)**
**Cuddington Community Primary School**


# Football

In football there are rules,
You play with size 5 balls.
It's really fun to watch,
Player can go up a notch.
You get 3 points if you win,
Be careful otherwise you'll break your shin.
A yellow card means a warning,
But some teams are really boring.

**Mathew Westrep  (10)**
**Cuddington Community Primary School**


# Hunger

My big round tummy,
When's dinner Mummy?
Come and see
What you and me
Should have for tea.
How about chips?
That will be nice for your hips!

**Connor McFadden  (10)**
**Cuddington Community Primary School**

# Laughter

The colour is yellow, like joyful moments,
People beam when they caress it.
If you ever relish it, it will taste like bananas,
As a sign of delight.
When you watch a funny comedy program
It will smell of custard pie, as they use it in shows.
It looks like a circus, imagined in your mind,
Don't fondle it, it will itch you like mad with comedy.
It probably would remind you of clowns,
The professionals.

**Harry Do  (10)**
**Cuddington Community Primary School**

# Darkness

The sun is suspended in the sky, bright and glorified.
Gradually, the sky's shades begin to deepen.
Everything fades and the sombre world opens onto the heavens,
So sable and shadowy.
Darkness comes, swallowing every object into its coal-blackness.
Eating traces of joy, it suppresses the Earth
And deepens the sleep of every living thing.
The world is starless, unlit and asleep.
Night has imprisoned the Earth.

**Bronwen Crowther  (10)**
**Cuddington Community Primary School**

# Laughter

Laughter is like a warm memory, it is filled with happiness,
Laughter is infectious, it is a box of warm popcorn,
Laughter is like a bubbly sweet fizzing on your tongue,
It is like a rainbow in the blazing multicoloured sky,
It's a box of tissues that makes you cry,
I take a breath and sigh, who am I?

**Abbie Harris  (10)**
**Cuddington Community Primary School**

# Fear

I hate darkness, it scares me in my sleep,
I dream of freaky monsters eating me like meat!

Suddenly I find confetti
And that's when I get sweaty.

So then I scream for Mum,
She thinks I shouldn't be scared, it's dumb.

But I know someone's waiting at night and his name is Fear,
He's the one who stole all of Dad's beer.

Luckily, now I sleep with a night light,
So I don't get such a fright.

And I still do see Fear,
But gladly he doesn't come near.

**Christopher Chipperton (10)**
**Cuddington Community Primary School**


# Darkness

A bitter darkness swallows you whole with the blinding of the dark air,
Eating the sun and chasing people away,
It pulls a spooky veil over your head,
The perplexing darkness gets daringly close,
All at once you're surrounded by the austere dullness,
A sparkling moon illuminates the sky,
Some winter sleet around me glows
With the reflection of the brightness,
I can see the river bank
Where the trees and bushes rustle,
Sunlight is bleaching the sky,
Darkness is racing away,
A modern day has arrived.

**Sacha Elledge (10)**
**Cuddington Community Primary School**

# My Dog

My dog is very cool and fun,
He's also very fast, watch him run.
I take him for walks to the park
But when he sees another dog he always seems to bark.
We always mess around inside and out,
We always play who's got the loudest shout.
At the end of the day when we all want to go to our beds,
We go to sleep with nice dreams in our heads.

**Martin Duddy  (10)**
**Cuddington Community Primary School**


# Shark

It swims through the sea
With its eyes open wide.
It looks out for food,
Swimming with the tide.

It finds its prey,
For its salty dinner.
It tears it up,
Now who's the winner?

**Jack Bates  (10)**
**Cuddington Community Primary School**


# Tutankhamun

I went on holiday to see the River Nile,
I wanted to know some facts so I looked in my file.
I went to the pyramids to see Tutankhamun,
Then saw a portrait of him in a tomb.
He always had hard working slaves,
But that was how it was in those days!

**Beth Leahy  (10)**
**Cuddington Community Primary School**

# Dogs

A fluffy friend to care,
Sometimes never share.
Intelligent little things,
You should check their backs for wings.
They can make a huge mess
As you would have probably guessed.
Love a good, long run,
For them it's great fun.
They know when you're down
You could give them a crown,
For being a cuddly bear
And for always being there.

**Chloë Brandon  (10)**
Cuddington Community Primary School


# Family Photo

Family photos are always a pain,
They always leave a shameful stain.
Sitting there smiling with my family around me,
I know I was only three,
But I still remember my mum, dad and me,
We were just a normal family.

**Ellie Bissell  (10)**
Cuddington Community Primary School


# Happiness

Happiness is children running round with joy,
Happiness is a baby's first word,
Happiness is winning a competition,
Happiness is passing your driving test,
Happiness is happiness.

**Scott Brown  (10)**
Cuddington Community Primary School

# The Beauty Of The World

The wind is a dragon
Clawing and biting at my face.
Swooping down from the heavens
His roar rattles the houses,
Breathing ice-cold fire.

The sea - a stallion
Galloping towards the beach,
Then rearing up and foaming down,
Stamping his hooves on the soft yellow sand,
Tossing his mane, then cantering back to the deep.

The clouds are sheep
In herds, wandering across the sky
Their fluffy white coats forming shapes
Or the black-coated rams
Darkening the sky with their rain clouds.

The night is a cat
Creeping up on you,
Eyes gleaming, watching your every move,
Padding on silent paws,
Then slinking away, when the morning comes.

Parrots are the dawn
Lighting the sky with their brilliant feathers,
Shaking away the darkness.
Their call waking you,
Welcoming you to the new day.

The phoenix - the sun
A glowing ball of fire,
Spreading its wings,
Sharing its warmth,
Bringing happiness to every heart.

**Alice Jeffers (10)**
**Danes Hill School**

# The Phoenix Of The Dawn

The day ended and the night began.
The night was as dark as ash,
It was also very cold.
It was lonely and silent as the sun went to sleep.

A spot of light appeared as the night passed.
The spot grew, now as large as an egg,
Then it was as big as a robin.
It grew and grew, until it was as large as a sea.

A glorious light of bright red and orange spread out.
It was as if a phoenix was stretching out its wings.
The phoenix was flying around gracefully like the warmth of the sun
Looking grand with its soft feathers.

While it was flying, the sun was glowing slowly,
While the sun glows, the dawn dies.
As the fire lights up, the phoenix was ready to rest.
Showing its last beautiful face
The dawn and the phoenix join the light.

**Sally Park  (10)**
**Danes Hill School**


# The Midnight Fear

A black cylinder coming towards me,
Wishing at this moment that I could not see,
As it gets closer I start to see the details,
A long black robe drooping like a sail.

His eyes are small red slits,
I see them as I sit,
A crumpled face like a bulldog,
But he kills like a warthog.

He floats across the land,
Bringing nightmares like grains of sand,
Then he feels weakened,
Then I can enjoy the night till day.

**Will Elbourne  (10)**
**Danes Hill School**

# Nature's Wonders

The wind is a dragon
Clawing and biting at my face,
Swooping from the heavens,
His roar rattles the houses,
Breathing ice-cold fire.

The sea is a stallion
Galloping elegantly across blue icy waters,
His anger is a tidal wave of foam,
The stallion cares for the world,
At night the sea is calm, for he is sleeping.

The parrot's plumage
Gives us rainbow rays,
A cocktail of colour lights us,
His squawk brings life to the world
As his golden orb rises from the horizon.

A cloud is a lamb,
Happily bouncing across the blue skies,
When he is sad the clouds darken,
One day he shall disappear
And visit you the next morning.

**Laura Galloway  (10)**
**Danes Hill School**

# The Sea

The sea, a most mighty leader
But when angry unmerciful.
His arms embrace the shore and devour it unforgivably
Like a lion feeding on its prey.

When satisfied he retreats,
The shore left in utter destruction,
Yet the sea, peaceful and calm.

The leader rests till his next call
Like a hibernating animal sleeping till spring.

**Thomas Eckl  (10)**
**Danes Hill School**

# Angel Of The Night

Night is kind and safe
Comforting you when you need her
Night makes me have sweet dreams
Driving all bad away from me
Looking after me in a motherly way.

The night is like an angel
With a face so rosy and fragile
Eyes so gentle and wise
With rose-red lips and perfect white teeth
Lips that never curl with anger.

Long, silky dresses adorn her
That swish slowly
While taking long sweeping steps
Her smooth hair swaying softly
Never leaving my side.

Night makes me think of calm,
Gentle, comforting things
Of the big wide world
But when I wake up I see nothing of her
For she is back in her house in the fluffy clouds.

**Alexandra Smith  (10)**
**Danes Hill School**

# The Sea Lion

The sea was an angry lion roaring in the night,
Its voice was a mighty roar echoing across the bay,
The lion was busy there lapping at the shore,
Its breath whistled round my house,
Forcing me under the covers.

The lion jumped here and there playing with its prey,
Its tail thrashed to and fro ripping sails to shreds,
The lion pounced and crashed against the cliffs,
And then, suddenly, the lion disappeared.

**Emma Reynolds  (10)**
**Danes Hill School**

# Sun, Sea, Clouds And Night

The sun is a fiery phoenix
Who looks down warmly on Earth,
His beautiful feathers shine like gold,
His elegant features happy and relaxed.

The sea is a white stallion
Galloping against the rocks,
His pounding hooves erode the cliffs
And crash against the waves.

Clouds are a flock of sheep,
Their white, woolly fleeces follow each other,
Stretching across the horizon
As far as the eye can see.

Night is a black panther,
His eyes shine brightly like stars,
He watches you from dusk to dawn,
Waiting to pounce!

**George Brighton  (10)**
**Danes Hill School**


# The Night Of My Content

Night is a warm comforting figure,
Whose face is hazy and calm.
He is ever watching,
An unseen guardian.

His hair is long and flowing.
Night moves as one with nature.
Long silky garments adorn his body.
His eyes are soft yet penetrating.

You may not see him
But he is there,
Always there.
He lives in a misty haven of soft grass
And wavy trees.

**Ben Allchurch  (10)**
**Danes Hill School**

# Nature's Poem

The wind is a dragon
Clawing and biting at my face,
Swooping from the heavens
His roar rattles the houses,
Breathing ice-cold fire.

The sea is a white stallion
Galloping at the rocks,
Many feel its great fury
But by the time people know it's too late.

The clouds are sheep,
White and fluffy in their grace,
Their bleat is the thunder,
Every now and then a new one is born.

The night is a giant bat
Swooping over the sky,
Its dark colour is threatening too the sun,
Many fear it throughout the land.

The dawn is a cat
Stalking away the darkness,
It is the bat's worst enemy,
It rules alongside the phoenix.

The sun is a phoenix
Associated with fire,
Its wings bring hope to many creatures,
It's reborn every day.

**Domenyk Turski  (10)**
**Danes Hill School**

# Nature's Moods

The cloud is a dove,
Flying above the green fields and blue ocean,
Its falling feathers are the many raindrops falling on the land,
It never stops its journey round the world.

The night is a bat,
Its leathery wings beating a cloud of darkness as it flies,
Creeping from the underworld to battle Dawn.

Dawn is a phoenix rising from the ashes each day,
Healing the wound of darkness,
Pulling away the blanket that covers the sun,
Exploding in colour.

The sea is a white stallion,
Galloping at the rocks,
All fear its white fury
As it storms the white sands.

The sun is a turtle
Plodding along, his shell lighting up the Earth,
It never gets tired, its light spreading hope,
One day the turtle will die, his grave the empty blackness.

**John McNally  (10)**
**Danes Hill School**


# Dawn

The dawn is a phoenix, the herald of Apollo,
Gliding across the sky like a heavenly chariot,
Kindling our hearts and filling us with zealous fire,
It marks the beginning of the day and lights up the sky,
The fiery trail it leaves is as beautiful as Venus.

**Adam Dayan  (10)**
**Danes Hill School**

# Nature's Wonders

*Sea*
The sea is a stallion,
Galloping across the shore,
Rearing up and crashing back down,
Swimming within the depths of the ocean,
Racing across the waves.

*Dawn*
Dawn is a phoenix,
Burning into the ashes,
Then coming back to life every morning,
It heals the wound of darkness,
By spreading its wings and showing its golden colours.

*Night-time*
Night-time is a bat,
Plunging the Earth into darkness,
By spreading its wings over the sky,
Draining the sun of all its colour,
When night-time ends dawn is ready to break free again.

*Clouds*
Clouds are swans,
Each one unique and different,
They move at their own pace,
Their fluffy feathers swaying in the breeze,
Flying peacefully across the sky.

**Katharine Burnett  (10)**
**Danes Hill School**

# My Midnight Fantasy

Night is a kind and comforting person,
She makes us feel safe,
While she cradles us in her arms,
She banishes all nightmares,
Leaving only the sweetest dreams,
Like an angel caring for you, she is relaxing,
Night's face is hazy and she has a gentle smile,
Her eyes are caring and moonlit,
She has a softly smiling mouth,
Her long jet-black hair blows in the wind,
Blending into the starry night,
Her robe sparkles like the stars flowing behind her,
Night moves majestically,
Floating on a bed of clouds,
When dawn breaks she returns to home,
Suspended from a star,
She falls asleep,
Contented that she has made a child's dream,
Safe and perfect.

**Katelyn Aitchison  (11)**
**Danes Hill School**


# The Moon

The moon glitters
Like a twirling disco ball,
Shines
Like a CD in the sky,
Glows
Like a cat's eyes on a dark road,
Beams
Like a headlight overhead,
Sparkles
Like a freshly polished ring,
Twinkles
Like a flickering fire in the dark.

**Catherine Keey  (10)**
**Danes Hill School**

# Nature's Moods

The dawn is a phoenix,
Arising from the ashes,
Healing the wounds of darkness,
He flies magically round the sky,
In chariots of golden fire.

The sun is a dragon,
Breathing hot fire,
Roaring heat down furiously,
Scaring people into the sheltering shade,
Burning our planet.

The wind is a swan,
Casting ripples across the water,
Gliding through the trees,
Gracefully whispering to the leaves,
Majestic in his flight.

The night is a cat,
Creeping slyly on to you,
Hunting for her innocent prey,
The alley cat jumps surprisingly out at you,
Wounding you until morning comes.

**Laura Koepke (10)**
**Danes Hill School**

# In The Blue

The angry sea crashes against the windswept shore,
Its white-capped waves dance in despair of their fate,
In its grey depths lies death and destruction,
The angry sea is sad.

The calm sea shimmers as it bathes in the sunlight,
Its waves sparkle as they kiss the golden shore,
In its azure depths is life and vitality,
The calm sea is happy.

**Catherine Thynne (10)**
**Danes Hill School**

# The Wind Is A Wolf

The wind is a wolf
Attached to the breeze,
Roaming the wild country,
Howling as it flies.

The night-time is a bat
Dying towards the fate of midnight.
His heartbeat is so slow,
We almost think he's dead.

The sea is a stallion
Frosting over the sea,
Defeating the waves
With its galloping hooves.

The snow is a polar bear
Ruling the Arctic land.
His soothing white fur
A vision in white.

The dawn is a phoenix
Rising from the ashes,
Gliding like a Chariot of Fire
Ascending towards sunrise.

**George Rexstrew  (10)**
**Danes Hill School**


# Lady Moon

The moon is a lady happily shining brightly,
The universe stares upon her beauty,
From Earth she is a glimmering star,
She is a light to guide from the dark,
The wolves howl deeply to her,
She is dead silent through the night sky,
She hides herself in day and reveals herself at night!

**Lucy Barrett  (10)**
**Danes Hill School**

# Daybreak

The dawn is a phoenix
Rising every morning,
Filling the world with light
After a night of darkness.

The sun is a parrot
Flying through the morning air,
The bright sunny colours
Filling the pale blue sky.

The clouds are doves
Gliding above the world,
Sweeping gracefully
In their fluffy white feathers.

The wind is a dragon
Clawing and biting at my face,
Swooping from the heavens, rattling the houses,
Breathing ice-cold fire.

The sea is a stallion
Galloping elegantly across the blue icy waters.
His anger is a tidal wave of foam
But at night the sea is calm, for the stallion is sleeping.

The night-time is an eagle,
His bright eyes glinting in the light of the moon,
Soaring through the night
In the brilliant darkness.

**Isabelle Griffin (10)**
**Danes Hill School**

# Night

Night is very mean
And cannot be seen.
He is cruel and scary,
So be wary.

Night makes you lonely and scared,
He will make you go further than ever you dared.
Night gives you nightmares and makes you think people are dying,
But that is when you start crying.

He will make your worst fears come true,
When you think he's watching you he is right on cue.
Night has a menacing face
And shall make you think you're a disgrace.

Night moves craftily and warily
And talks scarily.
His clothes are black
And will gaze heavily into your back.

Night is very mean
And cannot be seen.
He is cruel and scary,
So be wary.

**Balraj Gill  (10)**
**Danes Hill School**


# The Sea

The sea is a cold, violent creature,
Its body is dark and deep,
It destroys everything in its path with its wave-like arms,
It battles against the rocky shores,
It screams like an animal about to kill its prey,
And then it crashes down on its victim.

**George Parry  (10)**
**Danes Hill School**

# The Elements Of Nature

*Sea*

The sea is a white stallion
Racing across the sands of white,
Then retreating out of sight,
In the night-time he shall sleep,
Where he belongs at home in the deep.

*Sun*

The sun is a majestic lion,
Over this Earth he is king,
As he rises birds sing,
Over us all he glows with pride,
Friendly to all who stand by his side.

*Wind*

The wind is a fearsome wolf,
The wind is a wolf that scratches at doors,
Beware of his teeth and beware of his claws,
At night the wolf howls, his hunt was in vain,
But be sure to lock up as he'll try again.

*Dawn*

Dawn is a beautiful phoenix,
Dawn is a phoenix spreading its wings,
It has to be the most beautiful of things,
Reborn in the morning to light up the day
And when dark has gone then he'll soar away.

**Alexander Hurley (10)**
**Danes Hill School**

# In The Playground I Can See . . .

Cheerful Charlie charging,
Bashful Bertie barging.

Jealous George jumping,
Thoughtless Theo thumping.

Careful Kathy kicking,
Podgy Peter picking.

Harmless Helen hiding,
Skinny Simon sliding.

Hard-hearted Hannah hitting,
Neat Nancy knitting.

Lazy Lucy lying,
Sagacious Sue sighing.

Crafty Catherine crying,
Bewitching Bethy beating.

Zany Zoe's zooming,
Boring Ben booing.

Spiteful Sam spitting,
Hateful Helen hitting.

Silly Sophie sitting,
Eager Emma eating.

**Abigail Lawrence (10)**
**Danes Hill School**

# Animals Of Nature

*The sea is a stallion*

The sea is a free stallion,
Galloping towards the beach,
He rears just for fun,
Then returns to the watery deep.

*The sun is a lion*

The sun is a proud lion,
Glowing with pride over his kingdom,
Growling the heat down over it
And finally settling down to rest.

*The night is a bat*

The night is a vampire bat,
Spreading his wings over the sun,
Sucking the daylight from sight
And sharing his darkness with the world.

*The wind is a dragon*

The wind is a dragon,
Swooping from the heavens,
His roar rattles the houses,
Clawing and biting at my face.

**Kieran Copley (10)**
**Danes Hill School**

# The Magical Metaphoric Menagerie

The dawn is a parrot,
Full of colour and light,
Spreading its wings across the sky,
Bringing beauty to the Earth
And a smile to all who see it.

The sea is a stallion
Galloping across the waves,
Speeding through the water,
Rearing up onto the beach,
Then cantering back to the herd.

Each cloud is a cat
Moving gracefully through the sky,
But in a clap of thunder
And in a flash of lightning,
It could be on you with its claws.

The wind is a bear,
Seemingly gentle as a summer's breeze,
But when it turns
You see the monstrous beast of a hurricane,
Roaring all around.

Night-time is a bat
Swooping down from above,
Covering the Earth with its wings,
Protecting it from the sun,
Silently plunging the world into darkness.

**Nadia McLurcan (10)**
**Danes Hill School**

# In The Playground I Can See . . .

In the playground I can see . . .
Chirpy Charlie charging,
Barmy Bertie barging,
Ginormous George jumping,
Thin Theo thumping,
Clever Cathy kicking,
Perfect Peter picking,
Hilarious Helen hiding,
Stupid Simon sliding,
Big Ben burping,
Lazy Lydia lying,
Woeful William whining,
Sensible Sarah shining,
Horrid Hannah hurting,
Small Sophie squirting,
Enjoying Emma eating,
Bendy Becky beating.

**Sophie Vos  (10)**
**Danes Hill School**


# The Sun And Moon

*Sun*

When I enjoy the light
Of the sun, slowly
It melts away from our view.

*Moon*

A vital vitamin to life
That reflects an eerie
Light back home.

**Edward Barton  (10)**
**Ewell Castle Junior School**

# The Solar System

The moon is like
A snowball that
Keeps on rolling for eternity.

Saturn's rings are made
Out of crystals of
The solar system.

Inside the sun's beams
Are the souls of great
Warriors and heroes.

The stars were once
Flaming arrows that were
Shot up into the sky.

Each shooting star has
A heart inside it.

**Fred Kearey (10)**
**Ewell Castle Junior School**


# The Sun And The Moon

A powerful light
with sweaty and sticky
heat, so powerful.

An immaculate diamond
with a gentle and calm
light effect, but eerie.

Like a big orange giving
off heat and light,
pure vitality.

It's like a big ice cream
in the sky, but a
thousand times as cold.

**Oliver Stansfield (10)**
**Ewell Castle Junior School**

# The Sun And The Moon

A harsh light,
It is so hot,
Makes me lively,
Ready to get up.

Like a gentle glow,
A pearl in the sky,
It is time to end the day.

When the sun is in the sky
It gives out torch beams,
Which touch the ground.

When the moon is out
It is eerie, the silver veins
Make me frightened.

**Gregory Hughes (10)**
**Ewell Castle Junior School**

# The Sun And The Moon

The sun makes me warm
On the outside, and when
I'm down, the sun cheers
Me up again.

If I'm down, the moon
Makes me glow and
It makes me warm inside.

The sun is a-glowing
Mad fireball waiting to
Burst with furious light.

If my mum gets a very
Precious pearl.
It looks like the silvery moon.

**Sam Anderson (10)**
**Ewell Castle Junior School**

# The Sun And The Moon

*The sun*

The sun is harsh,
The sun is up,
The sun is powerful,
But not enough.

A warmth of happy
Love in space it beams
And glows half-way
Through its life.

*The moon*

Thoughts are back when
The moon is back in
The sky, it looks like
A cookie.

A ball in space not
Far away, it glows
In space like a
Humongous pearl.

**Sebastian Nowell (10)**
**Ewell Castle Junior School**


# The Sun/The Moon (Haikus)

*The sun*
The sun harpoons the
Earth with light, too brilliant
To observe or glimpse.

*The moon*
The moon has a soft
And gentle glow, like a big
Shiny, bright jewel.

**Max Northfield (10)**
**Ewell Castle Junior School**

# The Sun And The Moon

*The sun*
The sun, a huge
Football that
Hovers in the air

The powerful
Sunlight makes
You relax
And it makes
You boiling hot.

*The moon*
A huge demoded
That gives a
Gentle glow it
Makes me
Cry so much.

It gives its soft
Light out, day and
Night but you can't
See it in the day.

**Ismet Erdogan  (10)**
**Ewell Castle Junior School**


# What I Sell

I sell matches
I sell wood
I sell everything

I sell books
I sell paper
I sell everything

I sell some stick games
I sell ink
I sell everything for everyone.

**Nadeem Hussain  (7)**
**Goldsworth Primary School**

# In The Mine

Working as a trapper,
Working in the mine.
It's very unpleasant,
You never see sunshine.

Opening and shutting
Doors for air.
It's wet, damp and dark.
You wouldn't want to be there.

Sitting on the damp floor,
Feeling lonely and sad.
It's shivery and cold.
You would really think it's bad.

**Marion Stuttaford (7)**
**Goldsworth Primary School**


# Victorian Life

It was a dark place
It was not suitable for children
But they made children go
Down the mine to work.

**Mark Thornborrow (7)**
**Goldsworth Primary School**


# Mines

Nathan pulls boxes of coal,
It is hard for Nathan.
Nathan's friends don't help,
They never saw light.

**Nathan Guy (7)**
**Goldsworth Primary School**

# Mines

I feel so bored,
I am very tired,
I want to have fun.

I'm hungry and lonely,
Wishing I was loved,
I want to be free.

I'm in lots of pain,
And I'm very sweaty,
I want to be strong.

**Katie Marriott  (7)**
**Goldsworth Primary School**


# Mines

I was scared
It was dark and spooky
You could hear spooky noises
Benjamin knew it was the drawer,
Knew it was nearly time to open the door
He came puffing round the corner but
We could not have food.

**Ben Morrant  (8)**
**Goldsworth Primary School**


# The Rich

The rich are selfish,
The mums don't go to work.
The dads look cool,
The children have lots of toys
The baby is shouting.

**Jordan Appleyard  (8)**
**Goldsworth Primary School**

# Mines

I hate working in a mine,
I'd rather be at a school.
I want an education.
I'm thirsty, hungry and scared.

I barely get any money,
I'm struggling to move around.
I can't take it anymore,
I need to be free.

**Addison Bray  (8)**
Goldsworth Primary School


# Mines And Chimney Sweep

I work in a damp mine,
I'm cold and wet.
It's pitch-black apart from a dim light.
I work day and night.

I work all day,
Cleaning chimneys.
At the end of the day
My face is black and
I'm hungry.

**Abigail Mattingly  (7)**
Goldsworth Primary School


# A Victorian Poem

I am feeling sad
In the dark gloomy mine
Opening and closing the heavy door
All day long coal goes by.
I look forward to
A nice cup of tea.

**Amy Pearce  (7)**
Goldsworth Primary School

# Poor Miners

I am so hungry,
And I feel really sad.
I am so bored,
I wish I could have some fun.
I hate work.

I am really worried,
And I feel very scared.
I am very tired,
My knees are in lots of pain.
I hate work.

**Ruaridh Wallace (7)**
Goldsworth Primary School


# Victorian Mines

I work in the mine
I don't have much money
My knees are sore
All the time it is cold and dusty.
It's really hard work
I walk on my knees and legs.
At the end of the evening I am very tired.

**Alice Saunders (7)**
Goldsworth Primary School


# Miners

My sides are sore and scratched,
I'm scared and hurt.
It is dark and scary,
I'm scared and uncomfortable,
It is wet and cold and damp.

**Sammy King (7)**
Goldsworth Primary School

# Farewell Summer

Speckled veiny leaves
Floating softly to the ground
Swirling, twirling down.

Curly and crunchy
Tumbling, tumbling down
Drop without a sound.

Amber and crimson
Gold, scarlet and yellow too
Rustic and mottled.

**Sophie Jones  (9)**
**Manor House School**


# Autumn Senses

I feel a change in the air,
I see that all the trees are bare.

I hear the leaves crunch underfoot,
I smell the smoke from the burning wood.

I taste the apples that fall to the ground,
And wonder at the colours that surround.

**Laura Bushnell  (11)**
**Manor House School**


# Summer's Gone - Haikus

The leaves are crimson
They fall off trees in autumn
Floating to the ground.

Wind tossing the leaves
Scarlet leaves fall to the ground
Summer is going.

**Emily Williams  (10)**
**Manor House School**

# Lonely

Loneliness is pain beyond pain,
It swallows its victims in a timeless world
It looks like over-stretching darkness, with me in the middle.
You can't escape it.
The colour is of white, the colour of loneliness.
It feels like the wound of an ever-striking dagger.
It sounds like a shriek as high as the stars up in the night sky.
It tastes like cold blood
It smells like a mummy's rotting body
You can't escape it.

Once something steps up, you can't follow.
I couldn't.

**Amber Hearns (9)**
**Manor House School**


# Farewell Summer

The chill autumn air,
Leaves once glossy green, turn to brown,
Summer sun fading.

Bright shiny conkers,
Falling silently from the trees,
Spilling all around.

Chestnut conkers split,
They bounce to the ground.
Amber swirly veins.

**Maisie McCulloch (9)**
**Manor House School**

# Autumn Is Here

The leaves are falling down,
From every sort of tree.
Fluttering like butterflies
In a gentle breeze.

A new school year is starting
The birds are moving on,
Animals gather nuts for food,
You won't see them for long.

The garden world is closing down,
Everywhere's asleep.
Bonfire Night is coming round,
And Hallowe'en, trick or treats.

Dressing gown and slippers on,
Fireguard goes up.
Roasting chestnuts on the fire,
Hot cocoa in a cup.

**Florence Mills  (10)**
**Manor House School**


# Autumn Has Arrived

The autumn has arrived with a dismal thud
The leaves are whizzing round and round
Eventually crashing to the ground.
The fire crackles and burns great colours,
The fireworks fly high into the sky.
While we drink tea and watch them fly.
The crunchy leaves in the wood
The animals snuggled up in their warm nest.
Whilst thunderstorms are at their best,
Finally tomorrow's the day when witches cackle
'It's Hallowe'en!'

**Charlotte Ladd  (11)**
**Manor House School**

# Autumn's Grace

Summer's fading, oh so fast,
and winter's coming like a blast,
but in-between we have some space,
the autumn season with all its grace.

Colours so beautiful, how can it be,
oranges, yellows, what a sight to see,
these colours tumbling from the trees,
turning into piles of rustling leaves.

The days don't seem to be as long,
before you know it the daylight's gone.
It'll be Hallowe'en next week,
ghosts and monsters 'trick or treat?'

November brings firework night,
sparklers, fireworks, bonfires alight,
a bonfire which lights up the sky,
to remember that mean old Guy.

Sadly all the trees are bare,
no colours to be seen anywhere,
winter is just around the corner,
the grace of autumn will be no longer.

**Georgia Bean  (10)**
**Manor House School**


# Autumn

A cold shivering breeze dances through the trees
U nder the parked cars, swirl rainbow-coloured leaves
T he morning sky is inky-blue, as always before dawn
U ntil the sleepy winter sun gives an early yawn
M y cosy, woolly scarf and hat fit me like a glove but
N othing keeps me warmer than a warm September hug.

**Maddie Mortimore  (10)**
**Manor House School**

# Autumn

The rain and showers have awoken,
The shining sun has gone to sleep.
Although the autumn has begun,
Summer memories we shall keep.

The treetops are all different colours,
Orange, yellow, brown and red.
The leaves are twisting, turning down,
To make a crunchy, colourful bed.

Branches bear the very last fruits,
Apples, cherries, plums and pears.
To then be gathered in little baskets,
For us to enjoy in equal shares.

The weather is getting very cold,
The evenings are really dark.
People dress in coats and hats,
As they walk their dogs in the park.

Children are enjoying themselves,
In this new school year.
But autumn's coming to a close,
And winter's drawing near.

**Lucy Sharples  (10)**
**Manor House School**


# Autumn

Summer's over and autumn has come
Let's cheer as we see it run
Holidays are done with and school has begun
We all run out with our hats and gloves
The weather has changed from hot to cold
Twisting and twirling the leaves fall down.

**Komal Patel  (10)**
**Manor House School**

# Autumn

It is nearly the death of summer,
And winter is in the air.
As the autumn is coming,
I'm starting to prepare.
Now I'm getting worried,
Hallowe'en is nearly here.
The ghosts, the pumpkins, the vampires,
Are coming through the year.
All the animals hibernate,
And the rest are gathering food.
When the squirrels sleep
It puts me in the mood.
So I hurry to get outside,
When all the snow is falling
And I stay out there until
The day is nearly dawning.
Finally, spring is coming,
The trees are nearly grown.
All the bees are humming,
And I hope you've enjoyed this poem.

**Megan Laura Day  (11)**
**Manor House School**

# The Death Of Summer

The leaves are descending sadly in the swirling breeze,
Unhappy to come calling to the Earth.
While squirrels are frantically collecting nuts from the trees,
The children play happily in the pyramids of leaves.
Out wiggles the rake,
Say goodbye to all the fun,
Wait until the moon starts shining bright,
It's autumn tonight!

**Elinor Abraham  (10)**
**Manor House School**

# Favourite Colours

Some people like orange, some people like blue.
Some people like purple and bright yellow too.

Some people like red and some people like green,
But my favourite colour is one you've never seen.

My favourite colour is the best one of them all,
It can belong to big people and can belong to small.

My favourite colour is one you'll never see,
The only people who see it have the same problem as me.

My favourite colour is one you'll never find,
The only reason I see it is because I am blind.

**Katie Gilbard  (10)**
**Manor House School**


# Autumn

Autumn is the best time of the year,
Where summer goes and winter is near.

The damp smell of earth and leaves floating by
And the rain falling down from the top of the sky.

Up in the trees are colourful fruits,
And down below are children and their Wellington boots.

And those children are having conker fights,
And it's windy so some are flying their kites.

If we didn't have autumn, what would we do?
We'd have to hibernate with the animals too.

**Rachel Swatman  (10)**
**Manor House School**

# Animals

Once when I went out at night,
When I thought it wasn't very bright,
I went to go and get my candle,
But sadly it didn't have a handle.

I did have a fierce frown,
Because I dropped my candle down.
I woke all the animals up,
When a fox was having a pup.

An elephant was sleeping heavily,
On something very, very pebbly.
A mole was busy snoring, snoring,
It was getting sunny and warm, not pouring.

**Georgia Clark (8)**
Marist RC Primary School


# The Magic Pony

The magic pony is violet,
She can turn into a unicorn
And she has to go to pony school,
Although she has to wear uniform.

The unicorn has long eyelashes
And a beautiful silver horn.
Oh that lovely unicorn
It is almost dawn.

But in a flash . . . that lovely unicorn
Was a pony again.

**Charlotte Louise Manser (8)**
Marist RC Primary School

# It's Fun

It's fun to play in the sun,
We climb up the wall,
And then we start to fall.
We like to pull,
It's fun to play in the sun.

I went to run,
I got a bun,
I ran back to share my bun,
And then I went to go home.

After something rumbled
It was my tum.
I was hungry,
So I went to buy a big bun for just me!

**Marianna Difelice  (8)**
**Marist RC Primary School**


# Late One Night

Late one night at half-past twelve
My mummy's tights were stolen.
Then next morning she came back from work
To find her bottom was swollen.
So then my dad bought a new car
To take her to the doctor
But on the way something happened
And he drove off into a wall.
So he took out his mobile phone.
You'd think he would call the doctor
But instead he called the car repairer
He only cares about his car!

**Haydn Robinson  (7)**
**Marist RC Primary School**

# The Barmy Roman Army

The Roman army,
Has turned out to be barmy,
And our barmy Roman army,
Just can't lift a sword,
So the Celts are getting bored.

The emperor is feeling sad,
With his army doing bad,
And at the moment he is so sad,
That his Roman army has turned him mad.

Finally the barmy Roman army has stopped,
Because the emperor has thought of a plot,
He shall train his Roman army to clot
All the Celts with their swords.

In two years the emperor thought he had trained his Roman army,
But the Romans were still barmy,
They started playing darts with their swords,
And this made the emperor very mad.

**Ben Hodkinson (8)**
**Marist RC Primary School**

# Family And Friendships

Friendships are good
Swearing's bad
Mummy's glad
Sister's mad
Daddy's football crazy
And he's very lazy.
Daddy sleeps and never wakes,
Mummy's working, baking cakes.
I love my family, they are great.

**Sarah Ridley (7)**
**Marist RC Primary School**

# My Diary

*Monday*

On Monday
My mum goes crazy
She gets frustrated

*Tuesday*

On Tuesday
Mum loses her
Best pyjamas.

*Wednesday*

When it's teatime
Mum goes mad
Dad is ill.

*Thursday*

Now on Thursday
Auntie Liz has come to stay
Cos Mum and Dad have gone away.

*Friday*

Mum and Dad come home
And it's time for
Her to go.

*Saturday*

Finally it's Saturday
No school. Tomorrow surprise
Day with Dad to Wookey Hole.

*Sunday*

Finally Mum's calmed down
Dad is better
We can all go I suggested.

**Eloise Martin (7)**
Marist RC Primary School


# Friends And Family

Mummy and Daddy are friendly,
My brothers and sisters are not,
My cousins are very busy,
I really don't like them a lot.
But my friend is my best friend and I like her,
I like her a terrible lot!

**Daniella Grosso (8)**
Marist RC Primary School

# Walking In The Snow

Snowflakes falling pitter, patter, pitter,
Everyone is feeling very bitter.
Children building snowmen, who have got a hat,
Playing snowball fights - splat, splat, splat.
Wreaths are on the doorsteps, time for some singing,
*Ding, ding, ding,* the Christmas bells are ringing.
Wake up everyone, time to open some presents,
I got a pink palace, a queen and some peasants.
My brother got a cauldron and a toy wizard,
I really wish it would stop the blizzard.
My sister's got a toy baby hound,
Then my whole family came round.
My sister got a big perky . . .
When we ate the Christmas turkey.
Now we've had all the fun,
*Happy Christmas everyone!*

**Sophie Stadie  (8)**
Marist RC Primary School

# The Farm

Straw and hay fill the place.
The sound of cows as they graze.
The scarecrow stands lonely and sad,
Never stirring, silent as can be.
The horses gallop round and round,
Waiting for their dinner time.
The pigs rolling in the mud
Making a grunting noise.
The sheep baa in the field and watch the lambs jump around.
I play with my dolls that's what makes me glad.

**Elizabeth Joyce  (7)**
Marist RC Primary School

# Space, Space

Space, space
It's going for a race.
Space, space,
It's got a big fat face.
Space, space,
It's got a nice taste.
Space, space
It's got an alien case.

Space, space
It's got a black hole.
Space, space,
It's got no coal.
Space, space,
Cannot roll.
Space, space
Is very dull.

**George Marment (8)**
**Marist RC Primary School**


# Sweets Are My Favourite

Sweets, chocolate
They're my favourite.
Super chocolate,
Sherbet sweets
That's right.
The sherbet spills all over me.
I like toffee that's chewy
It gets stuck in my teeth.
I get annoyed, I can't get it out.
My favourites of them all are the toffees
Because I like trying to get them out.

**Jade Turner (7)**
**Marist RC Primary School**

# Football Crazy

I'm football crazy,
Chocolate mad!
Tennis, badminton,
They're all bad.

I'm cricket crazy,
Sweeties mad!
Baseball, hockey,
They are sad!

I'm football crazy,
Chocolate mad!
Tennis, badminton,
They're all bad.

I'm snooker crazy,
Sweeties mad!
Basketball, rugby,
They're all bad.

Football, cricket are the best!
Snooker, Formula One are the best of the rest!

**Alexander Beck (7)**
Marist RC Primary School

# Going To The Dentist

Dentists are horrible
And they smell
And I hate it when I have to have a filling
And they put air into my mouth.
The dentist makes me feel sick
Because of the leather seats.

**Mollie Young (7)**
Marist RC Primary School

# The Zoo

The zoo is a nice place to be
With all the nice sounds.
Even with a snake
That quivers all around.

How about a whale
Who swims in the sea,
Or even a snail
Which is very small to see?

**Natasha Lopez  (7)**
Marist RC Primary School


# My Family

My family is nosy,
My family is Italian,
My family is crazy,
My family is lazy,
My family is bonnie,
My family is jolly.
I have two sisters in my family
Called Celia and Letizia.

**Nadia Guarino  (7)**
Marist RC Primary School


# Look At The Ghost

Look at the ghost who looks at me.
He looks so scary!
Look at his terrifying face,
He's got braces that look like shoelaces.
Look at the way he flies,
Bedroom to bedroom and no one inside.

**Matthew Swan  (7)**
Marist RC Primary School

# In The Garden

In the garden
You will see
The laziest bumblebee.

In the garden
You will see
The prettiest bumblebee.

In the garden
You will see
The ugliest bumblebee.

**Claudia Harris  (7)**
**Marist RC Primary School**


# What Colour Is Blue?

Blue is my favourite colour:
The sea is blue,
The sky is blue,
The river is blue,
The pond is blue,
The flowers are blue,
My car is blue,
My cardigan is blue.

**Jessica Coady  (7)**
**Marist RC Primary School**


# Chatty Parrot

Chatty, chatty, chatty parrot,
Who always screams and always chatters.
He's lazy and makes terrible mistakes.
He's a silly parrot and he won't come back again.

**Kerri Brown  (7)**
**Marist RC Primary School**

# The Open Sea

Crashing waves bursting onto the shore,
The seaweed getting swept away,
The calm waves rippling on the sand,
The sea lion flowing across the sea,
The fishermen sitting by the shore,
In summer, splashing in the ocean,
The blue sea with peaked waves,
The splashing is always there!

**James Baskett  (7)**
**Marist RC Primary School**


# A Ghost Story

An enormous ghost sits on my sofa
He sits next to me and looks at me
I look at him too
I watch TV with him
I always see him on my sofa
My mum was terrified
She saw a flying chocolate bar
He was playing tricks on my mum.

**Jamie Melvin  (7)**
**Marist RC Primary School**


# Fantasy Football

The more goals they score,
The nastier the crowd.
The smashing strikes when they try to score.
The nasty tackles they always make,
When they always say it's truly a mistake.
When they save another goal
They say they've made history.

**Christian Beale  (7)**
**Marist RC Primary School**

# My Teacher

My teacher Mrs Martin
is truly a sunshine,
but all she ever talks about
is her fantastic relation.

My teacher Mrs Martin
is really very nice,
but hidden in her cupboard
are lots of little mice.

My teacher Mrs Martin
can talk and talk and say,
she chatters and chatters and chatters
every second of the day.

My teacher Mrs Martin
is very, very sweet,
all she does is tidy
and all she does is neat.

My teacher Mrs Martin
gets up early in the morning,
she goes into her husband's room
and finds he is snoring.

**Lucy Jarrett (9)**
**Marist RC Primary School**


# Yellow Things

Yellow is the hot beaming sun,
Yellow is the girls' school blouses,
Yellow is our literacy books,
Yellow hay lays in horses' stables,
Sweetcorn is very yellow,
And yellow is like the bright school light.

**Katie Corbett (7)**
**Marist RC Primary School**

# Colours

The colour blue
Is the colour of the sky.
The colour green
Is the colour of the grass.
The colour pink
Is the colour of my cheeks.
The colour yellow
Is the colour of the sun.
The colour brown
Is the colour of chocolate.
These are the colours that I like
But my favourite colour of all is
The colour red, because
It is the colour of Santa's hat.

**Amy Cross  (7)**
**Marist RC Primary School**


# Summer And Night

The acorns are falling,
The tree is talking.

The birds are singing,
The nest is tweeting.

The worms are walking,
The hens are talking.

The flowers are dancing,
The sun is rising.

The moon is shining,
The stars are flying.

**Daniel Hill  (7)**
**Marist RC Primary School**

# The Sea

The sea
Is extensive, it stretches for miles
The sand makes us smile
The water is a reflection of the blue sky above
Seagulls sing and fly and hover above
I am lying on the beach
I am lying on the sand
I write with my hand
So I am talking to a crab
Lying on my left
Lying on my right
I play alot on the sand
I laugh alot in the water
I think alot for the beach.

**Joseph Fernandes  (11)**
**Marist RC Primary School**


# Aliens And Ghosts

Aliens are slimy,
Ghosts are hairy,
Aliens are scary,
Ghosts are chatty,
Aliens are skinny,
Ghosts are crazy,
Aliens are muddy,
Ghosts are gloomy,
Aliens are silly,
Ghosts are frightening,
Aliens are smelly.

**April Coady  (7)**
**Marist RC Primary School**

# Springtime

I love the beautiful springtime
I love to play outside
I love to smell the springtime smells
When springtime comes.

When springtime comes
I like to hear the sound
Of the birds singing as they fly around
I like to feel the breeze when springtime comes.

My father is mowing the lawn today
So I cannot go out and play
I wish I could just smell the smell
The smell of springtime when it comes.

I love to smell the scented flowers
I love to watch the huge, fat trees
I love to watch them blowing in the breeze.

When springtime is here
It makes me want to dance
When springtime is here
It makes me want to prance.

**Milly Lowther (9)**
**Marist RC Primary School**


# Aliens

Aliens are mean,
Aliens are nasty,
Aliens are slimy,
Aliens are skinny,
Aliens are clever,
Aliens are ghastly,
Aliens are sneaky,
Aliens are cheeky,
So if you see an alien, don't try and fight,
If I were you, I'd scream and take flight!

**Louis Mamet (7)**
**Marist RC Primary School**

# The Weather

I like rain, rain is fun
Splashing in my wellies
Waiting for the sun.

I like sun, sun is fun
Waiting for the barbecue
Ready to be done.

I like wind, wind is fun
Flying my kite
'Til the wind has gone.

I love snow, snow is cool
Ice-skating
On the frozen pool.

I like the cold, cold is cool,
Standing in the forest
With hat and snowball.

**Sarah Callan  (8)**
**Marist RC Primary School**


# Disgusting Dinners

Throwing food everywhere,
all the children don't really care.
Sausages, potatoes, nuggets and chips,
horrible pudding with strawberry bits.
Dinner ladies running about,
trying to find a way out.
Sausages burnt, nuggets undercooked,
the head teacher came and looked.
She didn't have time to stop and stare,
as all the food flew in her hair.
There were bits of food everywhere,
none of the children really care.

**Katy Richards  (10)**
**Marist RC Primary School**

# My Favourite Pet

My favourite pet is Scooby,
He is orange but he has white stripes around him,
And I love him very much.

Scooby is a jolly pet,
Even though he's naughty,
And I love him very much.

I am so touched that he likes me,
I know because he purrs in my ear,
And I love him very much.

I am hungry when I smell the herbs,
I smell them because he walks in the flowers,
And I love him very much.

I feel warm as he snuggles me,
He always purrs as well,
And I love him and he loves me.

**Dervla Hynes (8)**
**Marist RC Primary School**


# Last Day At School

We go into school in the morning,
Lots of us are still yawning.
In assembly the teacher looks around,
Most of us are sitting on the ground.
We talk a lot in assembly,
People think we're at Wembley.
We go out of the hall,
Tired, we can hardly stand up tall.
At break no one can understand,
Why we're sitting on the ground.
When we finished the day Mum said,
'Why are you so tired?'

**Liam Jarrett (10)**
**Marist RC Primary School**

# Colours Of The Rainbow

A rainbow is a beautiful sight,
especially when it shimmers in the light.
Seven colours in it, oh so bright,
a rainbow is a beautiful sight.

The first colour is red, ever so deep,
that it makes you never want to go to sleep.
It is like thick blood so, so fresh
trickling down someone's flesh.

Next there is orange,
the colour of a golden sun
that brings lots of joy
and lots of fun.

Yellow is next in the line,
so soft and so fine.
It is the colour of flowers all in a row,
gleaming in the sun with a bright little glow.

Then there is green,
as bright as the grass,
moving in the strong wind,
ever so fast.

After there is a soft blue,
the colour of the sky,
moving across with the little clouds
all saying bye.

Next there is indigo
like the deep blue sea,
travelling past,
with a strange flow.

Violet is the last one,
full of glee and fun,
the colour of a purple balloon,
floating in the sun.

**Letizia Guarino (10)**
**Marist RC Primary School**

# A Day At The Seaside

Sparkling waters, golden sands
People playing in the sun
Building sandcastles under the trees
Families eating picnics on the beach
Blue skies, yellow sun
Happy faces all over the beach
Everybody is having a lovely day at the seaside.

**Sean Feline (10)**
**Marist RC Primary School**

# The Beach

It's not always warm
But it's fun
Huge and enjoyable
For everyone
The sea goes out as far
As the eye can see
The water's as cold as ice can be
I feel excited, happy and stunned
Like the water is taking me out to sea
Away from England
A whole different world for me.

**Anna-Maria Grosso**
**Marist RC Primary School**

# Daisy

There was a girl called Daisy,
Who was a bit crazy,
She jumped off a rock,
And fell in a dock,
But now she's very lazy.

**Kieran Comer (11)**
**Marist RC Primary School**

# My Bedroom

My comfortable bedroom,
Is very colourful,
It's spectacular, superb and stunning,
As pink as a pig,
As peaceful as an empty playground,
Mysterious, magical, mythical,
As warm as fire,
My delightful, dreamy bedroom,
Is an imaginative place to be.

**Catherine Ferris (10)**
Marist RC Primary School

# The River

The river
A moving piece of colourless liquid
Beautiful, shiny, magical
As wet as a cold bath
It flows like a piece of long silk
Its like being on a roller coaster
The river.

**Oonagh Powell (10)**
Marist RC Primary School

# Dogs

Dogs are yappy,
Always happy.
They're full of fun,
They always run.
Energetic, excited and entertaining,
As high as a kite.
They have pleading eyes,
You cannot deny.

**Olivia Lynch (10)**
Marist RC Primary School

# The Canal

The canal glistens and shimmers like a crystal mirror,
reflecting the trees and singing birds above
like a carpet of bright glitter.
The sun shines over it making the shiny pattern
which gleams across like a fairy sprinkling her magic.
The fish swimming under are colourful and their scales sparkle
as they glide through the water.
In the spring ducks float out onto the crystal water
to teach their little ducklings to swim.

**Ellie Wiczling  (10)**
**Marist RC Primary School**


# Happiness

Happiness is blue like a river flowing gracefully through the valley.
It sounds like the birds chirping happily in the treetops.
Happiness smells like a cake in the oven waiting to be eaten.
It tastes like the cherry on top of a sugary mince pie.
Happiness looks like all the children playing in the park.
It feels like the silky fur on a cat.
Happiness reminds me of a multicoloured rainbow shining high
in the sunlight sky.

**Scott Santos  (10)**
**Marist RC Primary School**


# Sadness

Sadness is a colour of blue and white,
Sadness is a sea of darkness,
Sadness is a ghost, feasting on your happy soul,
Sadness is a deadly virus in your eyes just waiting to come out,
Sadness is a shadow covering all your happiness,
Sadness is a secret agent with a mission to make your life a misery.

**George Worsfold  (10)**
**Marist RC Primary School**

# What My Life Is Like

My brother Nick who's always sick
My brother Mike who I don't like
My mum drinks rum
My dad's so mad
And that's what my family is like.

I have some neighbours to the right
They always get into a fight
One's called Sue who always needs the loo
One's called Sam who really hates ham
Their mum is called Rosie who's very dozy
Their dad's called John who hates the lights on
That's what my neighbours are like.

I have a dog and a cat that's dumb
For some reason my cat likes plums
That's what my pets are like.

I've introduced you to everyone
Who I think are very dumb
And that's what my life is like.

**Harry Burt  (10)**
**Marist RC Primary School**

# Silence

Silence is white like a blank piece of paper,
It sounds like a room of mouths, but saying nothing.
It tastes like an empty, dry mouth,
It smells of cake that no one will eat,
It looks like a book with no words,
It feels as smooth as silk,
It reminds me of clapping with only one hand.

**Matthew Stanbrook  (10)**
**Marist RC Primary School**

# Easy-Peasy Lemon Squeezy

Hack into the webmaster huh?
So easy!
Learn to cook gourmet food?
Easy-peasy!
Say supercalifragilisticexpealadocious two
Hundred times backwards?
Easy!
Fit myself into a spy camera,
At crush depth under
The sea huh?
Peeaaassssyyy!
Jump into a pool of acid?
Eaasssyyy!
Win the lottery?
Easy!
Eat school dinners?
What?
You're mad! That'd
Kill you!

**Patrick Letch (11)**
**Marist RC Primary School**


# Puppies

Puppies
Are fun and full of joy
Plant pots and slippers
They love to destroy
They're as cheeky as a monkey
And they're cool and funky
They're cute, dinky and always cheerful
They're clumsy, funny and very playful
Puppies
Are the best
And they never, never rest.

**Sheryl Jared (10)**
**Marist RC Primary School**

# Ants

Ants marching to and fro,
hiding in the grass below.
In the grass they make their nest,
then they sit down to rest.
They march and march all day long,
as the birds sing their song.
They work as hard as me and you,
then they stop to have a chew.
They carry things like straw and hay,
then they stop to have a play.

**Lucy Butler (10)**
Marist RC Primary School


# Summer

Summer
Summer
It's finally here, lovely flowers
Beautiful trees
Wondrous grass, lovely and green
Tasty fruits, lovely and ripe
Freshly picked from the veggie patch.

**Thomas Rhodes (10)**
Marist RC Primary School


# Rain

Rain is cold when it hits your head,
It keeps you awake in your bed.
Pitter-patter, pitter-patter all day long,
Then the rain stops, the sun comes out
And the children are playing all about.

**Sam Walrond (10)**
Marist RC Primary School

# Darkness

Darkness isn't kind like a friend called Beth,
Darkness is as cold as death,
Darkness hasn't got a sound,
Darkness is easily found,
Darkness is a killer of the light,
Darkness feels like a wolves' bite,
Darkness feels like coldness running down your spine.
Darkness is like being pricked by a needle from a pine,
Darkness is blacker than black,
Darkness is like having the Devil on your back.

**Marcus Newall (10)**
**Marist RC Primary School**


# The Crazy Monkey

There was a monkey who lived in the zoo
and when you came along he always said, 'Boo!'
The adults would jump and the children would bump
and so would the keepers too.
He would joke all day and laugh all night
then fly his kite, whilst the others would fight.

**Isabel Allan (10)**
**Marist RC Primary School**


# Fun

Fun is the colour of a *golden* sunshine
Fun sounds like children laughing
Fun tastes like a packet of sweets
Fun smells like sweet candyfloss
Fun looks like a blue sky
Fun feels like the heat of the sun
Fun reminds me of happy children.

**Jack Gosling (10)**
**Marist RC Primary School**

# Hate

Hate is black like the cruel Devil,
Eating you up inside,
It sounds like a pack of fierce greyhounds,
Barking and biting at you every second,
It feels like boiling hot tar,
Burning and glistening mercilessly,
It tastes like chilli sauce,
Burning and stinging at your tongue,
It smells like blood, sickening and deadly,
It reminds me of the Devil, cruel and evil.

**Peter Baskett (10)**
**Marist RC Primary School**


# Trees

Trees stand high and tall,
Some are old, thin or small.
They are like tall sticks,
Or a pile of bricks.
Trees make me feel
Like the world is growing without me.

**James Grady (10)**
**Marist RC Primary School**


# People

Black and white
they're all a different height
some are tall
some are small
but none are so individual as you
that's because we're all different in what we do.

**Laura Sessions (10)**
**Marist RC Primary School**

# What Is The . . . Sun?

The sun is as hot as fire,
It is as enormous as an elephant,
The sun is as curled as a ball,
It is as clear as a light,
The sun is as tall as a giraffe,
It is as shiny as a diamond,
The sun is as pretty as a bouquet,
It is as fit as an athlete,
The sun is as soft as cotton wool,
It is as beautiful as a rose.

**Eleni Habib**
Marist RC Primary School


# Hip Hop

Hip hop is the best
I think it comes from the west
It has an excellent beat
And the rhythm sweet
It's a new music race
People can't keep up with the pace
I think it's worth listening too
But how about you?

**Raj Majithia**
Marist RC Primary School


# Suzie's Jacuzzi

There was a young lady called Susie,
Who liked to have a snoozie,
When she woke up,
She saw a small pup,
And took her in her jacuzzi.

**Lavinia De Vivo**
Marist RC Primary School

# God's Living Creatures

The caterpillar feeds on leaves,
Roughly, the eagle swoops on prey,
A snake bites its food and swallows it whole,
People eat almost anything,
Horses eat meat and straw,
Butterflies flutter in the breeze,
Snails slither simply,
Chickens cluck all day,
Swans drift upon lakes,
Spiders spin a web for a home,
Horses gallop in the breeze,
A bird's home is a nest,
Owls are said to be wise,
Wolves are predators that hunt through the night,
Bees gather pollen from flowers,
A mouse's house is a hole in the ground . . .
And a house is a home for me!

**Dan Letch (9)**
**Marist RC Primary School**


# Illnesses

I wouldn't like to have diabetes,
And inject insulin into myself twice a day,
I wouldn't like to have diabetes,
Because it never goes away.

I wouldn't like to have cancer,
Because you have to have an operation,
I wouldn't like to have cancer,
Because it takes over like an invasion.

I wouldn't like to have asthma,
Because you get attacks,
I wouldn't like to have asthma,
Because of all the facts

*I don't want to get an illness!*

**Josie Turner (10)**
**Marist RC Primary School**

# Horror

Fear is midnight blue like
The pitch-black nights with
My shivering breath in front of me.

It sounds like the call of
An owl, or the total silence
Of a deserted beach in the
Early hours of the morning.

Horror feels like a cold,
Spine-chilling, tickling spider
Crawling up my leg.

It tastes like a sour, bitter
Lemon or a glass of sharp
Salty water on the tip of my tongue.

Fear looks like the windows
Freezing up and a cold wind
Blowing down the chimney
On a cold, lonely winter's night.

**Stefan Brown  (10)**
**Marist RC Primary School**


# Hate

Hatred is black like death, seething inside you,
Eating you up,
It sounds like a cannon, booming inside you,
It tastes like mud, squirting inside your mouth,
It smells like rancid milk when it is forced up your nose,
It looks like a bottomless pit,
It feels like someone throttling you,
It reminds me of disappointment.

**Amy Weddell**
**Marist RC Primary School**

# Love Is . . .

Love is red and passionate,
Love is the sound of the birds singing,
Love is the taste of a sweet box of chocolates,
Love is the smell of roses,
Love is the look of a bouquet of red roses,
Love feels like a hot bath,
Love reminds me of Valentine's Day.
Love is . . .

**Claire McCarthy**
**Marist RC Primary School**


# Sadness

Sadness is blue like a cold, wet day in winter,
It sounds like babies screaming and children crying,
It tastes like the sour taste of lemon,
It smells like you've just been sick,
It looks like a devil, waiting to gobble you up,
It feels like gone off honey,
It reminds me of my grandad dying.

**Sam Morreale (11)**
**Marist RC Primary School**


# Winter

Winter is silver like stars shining,
It sounds like sleigh bells jingling,
It tastes like warm Christmas dinner in my tummy,
It smells like needles falling off my Christmas tree,
All the snow looks like a blanket across the grass,
It feels jolly with all the children laughing and playing happily,
It reminds me of my stocking when it is full of presents.

**Rosie Antoniazzi (10)**
**Marist RC Primary School**

# The Fat Man Tale

This is the tale of the fat man,
Who sat on the couch all day,
He drank beer and ate pizza,
Watching TV was his way.

Now, one day, when he was at home,
He knew that he was alone,
He took out a packet of crisps,
And ripped it to bits,
But he knew that his new tuxedo wouldn't fit.

As he plonked himself on the sofa,
He knew that his weight would double,
*But how will that harm me?* he asked himself,
But oh gosh was he in trouble!

He fell to the floor with a plop,
His belly went pop,
He gave out a wail,
And went all pale,
And this is the end of the fat man tale.

**Jack Bousfield (10)**
**Marist RC Primary School**


# Little, Old Squirrel

The small squirrel sniffs like a dog,
He runs as fast as a toddler,
He is nibbling acorns,
He is munching like the poor of the world,
He is sweeping his tail side to side,
He is twitching and itching like a cat,
His fluffy fur is pushed forward as he scurries,
He walks twitching his fluffy tail,
He sniffs again like a dog.

**Alice Hurl (9)**
**Marist RC Primary School**

# Aeroplane

The aircraft hurtles along the runway at breakneck speeds,
It achieves lift-off,
Soaring through the air with the greatest of ease,
Suddenly, like a hawk it dives,
But then it zooms upwards to Heaven,
It pulls off a loop,
Then it's an owl swooping smoothly,
Landing on long green grass,
I'm exceedingly proud of my paper aeroplane!

**Andrew Marken (9)**
Marist RC Primary School


# Boredom

Boredom is grey like the colour of rain,
It sounds like a pencil scratching on paper,
Boredom tastes like tap water when I want Coke,
It smells like a build up of dust,
Boredom looks like an old school classroom,
It feels like the school desks,
Boredom reminds me of maths!

**Veronica Fragassi (11)**
Marist RC Primary School


# My Brother's A Soldier

Once my brother was a soldier,
But then he got shot in the shoulder.

They took him to the Medical Centre,
And tried to make it better.

Then the germs rested in his shoulder,
And now there's no more soldier.

**Brendan Conlan (9)**
Marist RC Primary School

# Where Is Your Homework?

'Where is your homework? It should be in today,'
'I went to the dark side of the moon Miss,
And when I came back it was late afternoon Miss.'
'So why didn't you do it then, why not then?'
'Well, you see an alien came for tea Miss,
And it took my bedroom key Miss.'
'Then why didn't you do it in another room?'
'There is no other room Miss,
But we may be getting one soon Miss.'
'Why didn't you do your homework outside?'
'The cars were blocking the grass Miss,
So you see Miss I couldn't do it that fast, Miss.'
'How about the car, you can do it in there?'
'No, I can't you see, it was filled with boxes Miss,
And the boxes were filled with wild oxen Miss.'
'How about you do it at school then?'
'Well, all right Miss, I will!'

**Sarah Smith (9)**
**Marist RC Primary School**


# What Happened To Alice?

Tweedledum and Tweedledee,
Soon they will see,
A little girl called Alice, pretty as can be,
She went wandering in the wood one day,
Not knowing what she'll find,
Soon she'll face decisions she'll have
To make up her mind.
Along the way, she'll meet a rabbit,
And a very quarrelsome queen.
By the end of the day Alice is very bored,
All she wants to do is go home,
But she cannot find the key!

**Catherine Wort (10)**
**Marist RC Primary School**

# Isla's Castle

At Krum Castle,
In Aberdeen,
There is a beautiful sight to see,
For in there lies Lady Isla as peaceful as can be.
A tragic story, yes, oh yes,
A story that will break your heart,
For that is what it did for me,
Go through at least a hundred rooms,
Past the servants and their brooms,
In the dungeons you will see,
Isla's private nursery,
In the dust and in the damp,
Where only rodents play now.
A little carving on the wall saying neatly,
'Isla's the bold princess 1809.'
A whole year before her little life ended,
And now people who visit always say,
They can still hear her carving her name with pride.

**Molly Raymer**
**Marist RC Primary School**


# The Famished Dragon

In a cave bursting with treasure,
Lies a dragon, full of pleasure,
He guards it as if it was a child of his own,
Anyone who disturbs him will be burnt to the bone,
The dragon comes out of his cave,
For a peep and maybe to gobble down a few sheep,
The dragon spots the sheep, his lunch, and
Bites into it,
*Crunch!*

**Joseph Norman (10)**
**Marist RC Primary School**

## Sparkling Snow Floating Down Through The Air

In the snow I love to laugh
As the snow comes floating down,
It floats from the sky, like fairy dust,
Falling into my hair.
Snowflakes land on my hand
And break like little crumbs.
The snow is cold and turns me to ice,
But the snow is still so nice.
The sun came out and the snow went away
Melting day by day.
But I'll remember that day
The snowiest day of the year.
I guess it's gone to the Arctic now,
It's gone, gone for food,
It'll come back next year,
I think.

**Molly Breeden**
**Marist RC Primary School**


## Can You Fly?

Have you ever wondered if you can fly?
Why not simply give it a try?
Soar like a plane,
That would be my game,
Or hover like an eagle,
That would be illegal,
Don't be scared, it's easy to do,
It'll be no fun without you,
So have you ever wondered if you can fly?
All you have to do is give a great leap,
And soon you will be soaring over those sheep,
Fly over the moon, see you soon,
So fly, fly, fly, give it a try,
It's not as if you are going to die.

**Oliver Ryan (9)**
**Marist RC Primary School**

# What Is The Moon?

The moon is a chunk of Swiss cheese
On a dusky chopping board,
It is a silver button on a black cloak,
It's a cream netball being passed
Around a gloomy court,
The moon is a paper boat floating
On a muddy puddle,
It is a round ivory box trapped
Inside a dark wardrobe.
What is the moon to you?
A futile thing that waxes and wanes
Or something you admire?
Think!

**Anna Creagh-Chapman  (9)**
**Marist RC Primary School**


# What Is A Tiger?

A tiger is as stripy as a zebra crossing,
A tiger is like a powerful orange zebra,
A tiger is like a bigger version of a cat,
But it kills for its living so it can eat.

**Harry Duddy  (9)**
**Marist RC Primary School**


# The Sea

It's like the world's biggest bathtub,
Like a giant jacuzzi overlapping the world's shore,
With waves coming, humans bobbing,
Massive, navy and sun-sparkling light.

**Elena Hookins  (9)**
**Marist RC Primary School**

# Drifting Clouds

Clouds are balls of cotton wool,
Hovering up above,
Clouds are pink candyfloss,
Floating at the sunset.
A bubble bath,
Drifting through the thin blue air,
A vast storm of snowballs,
Thrown up in the open sky,
A colossal swarm of bubbles,
Tossed into the heavens.

**Brooke Collins**
**Marist RC Primary School**


# Small Squirrel

The small squirrel,
Scampers and scurries,
As quick as lightning,
Gathering nuts for winter,
The wind blows,
As cold as ice,
His warm, fluffy fur,
Is like a radiator,
To warm him,
Through the cold winter months.

**Gabriella Giles**
**Marist RC Primary School**


# A Tree

A tree is like broccoli but much bigger,
A large green object that stands up,
A tall plant with leaves,
A tree is like a gigantic branch.

**Laura Tabiner (9)**
**Marist RC Primary School**

# What Are Clouds?

What are clouds?
They are puffs of candyfloss,
They are a giant bubble bath travelling round and round,
They are huge snowballs thrown into the sky,
They are bubbles hovering in thin air,
They are gigantic white shells drifting
Around the heavenly ocean.

**Georgina Haslam**
Marist RC Primary School


# The Sea

The sea is a blue calm pool,
It is a gigantic blue bath,
It is full of sand,
It is like a giant lake full of
Deep, deep water,
The sun is making the sea *hot* like fire,
It is as blue as the sky,
The sand is as brown as a dog.

**Chereece Chambers  (9)**
Marist RC Primary School


# The Big Moon

The moon is like a white football kicked in the sky,
A huge white bubble floating in the sky,
It is a big snowball in the sky,
A white mosquito bite,
A huge white sun such as a white clock spinning,
A white candle lighting the sky.

**Mark Gouveia**
Marist RC Primary School

# Tiny Tony

Tiny Tony,
Taught tiny Tom
To play
Table tennis
It's great fun.

Tiny Tony,
Told tiny Tom,
The actions
To play
It's great fun.

Tiny Tom,
Hit tiny Tony,
With the ball
On his head,
It's great fun.

**Oliver Thompson  (7)**
**Marist RC Primary School**


# The Sea

The sea is like a giant bath
Lapping different shores.
The sea is like a massive swimming pool,
Embracing the countries of the world,
The sea is like a huge jacuzzi,
Bubbling and splashing the land.
The sea is like an enormous blob of blue paint,
Swirling its colour on the globe.

**Sacha Femandes  (9)**
**Marist RC Primary School**

# Football

Football, football,
Is a game,
Football, football,
Is a pain.
Football, football,
Is the rain,
Football, football,
Down the lane.
Football, football,
Is insane,
Football, football,
Is fame.
Football, football,
Is very crazy.
Football, football,
Is very lazy.
I like football!

**Ashley Rannie (8)**
Marist RC Primary School


# What Is A Pufferfish?

A small spiky football,
Pushing its way through the sea,
A lychee
Floating amongst coral reefs,
A round spiky pin cushion,
Poisonous and deadly,
A sharp cactus,
Bobbing in its ocean home.

**Max Brown (9)**
Marist RC Primary School

# A Busy Bee's Life

In the hive the bee wakes up in his hexagon bed,
He takes off his pyjamas and puts on his black and yellow suit,
He says goodbye to his bee friends like Mike, Tim and Ed,
Then sets off to get honey from a flower bed,
He flew to the tulips, and the poppies and daisies,
Then got some pollen from a crazy daisy,
On the journey back home, he got caught in a spider's web,
He called for help, then the spider heard him yelp.
The spider came and unravelled him, then the bee
Flew back home and shared the pollen with the rest.

**Susan Shiel-Rankin (9)**
**Marist RC Primary School**


# The Moon

As white as a blob of white paint on pale blue paper,
It is a round, white ball in the sky,
It is a round cheese thrown into the heavens,
It is a round bowl tossed into the air,
As a white lid in the sky,
It is a mint thrown up above.

**Pietra Morello (9)**
**Marist RC Primary School**


# The Moon

The moon is like a saucepan of milk in the moon's kitchen,
The moon is like a white football in the moon's goal,
The moon is like an Mint Imperial in the moon's corner shop,
The moon is like a snowball in the moon's garden,
The moon is like a blob of white paint in the moon's DIY shop.

**Jack Rundle (9)**
**Marist RC Primary School**

# Clouds

Clouds are puffs of candyfloss floating up above,
Clouds are a bubble bath in the sky's bathroom,
Clouds are puffs of dragon smoke,
Clouds are snowballs being thrown in the *enormous* sky,
Clouds are bubbles blown from a giant's wand.

**Ella Worsfold (9)**
**Marist RC Primary School**


# Creamy Clouds

A cloud is like a massive drift of snow tossed up into the air,
A cloud is like an enormous fluffy pillow,
A cloud is like candyfloss floating in the heavens,
A cloud is like giant bubbles in the skies above,
A cloud is like colossal chunk of whipped cream in the heavens.

**Isabelle Hurl (9)**
**Marist RC Primary School**


# The Best Turtle

A turtle is a large ocean shell on the beach for 150 years!
It's like a tiny walking boat, that has never been rowed,
It's a massive snail shell, glossy and green,
It's like a walking sun, that never rests.

**Billy Robbins**
**Marist RC Primary School**


# The Shining Sun

As gold as a lid from a milk bottle,
As yellow as a pineapple from a market,
As yellow as a rubber thrown into the sky,
As yellow as a lemon.

**Rosalba Morello (9)**
**Marist RC Primary School**

# What Is The Moon?

A colossal piece of Edam cheese thrown into space,
It's like a white football kicked up so high,
It is like a silver coin tossed into the heavens above,
A gigantic piece of white chocolate left in the atmosphere,
An enormous jaw breaker flung into the stratosphere.

**Samuel Glennon (9)**
**Marist RC Primary School**


# Excitement!

Excitement is multicoloured like a bright, blending rainbow.
Excitement sounds like a wonderful fairground racing around my mind.
Excitement tastes like soft, creamy ice cream melting in my mouth.
Excitement smells like crunchy, juicy sweets.
Excitement feels like a soft, squishy cushion.
Excitement reminds me of enchanting love.

**Emily Gay (9)**
**Nutfield Church CE Primary School**


# Hunger

Hunger is like brown melted chocolate
Hunger sounds like a huge stomach gurgle
Hunger tastes like a great big banquet
Hunger smells like a smelly fish at the pier
Hunger feels like a scaly, slithery snake
Hunger reminds me of marshmallows over a fire.

**Luke Bellars (9)**
**Nutfield Church CE Primary School**

# Anger

Anger is a really dark purple like a sparkling shooting star.
It sounds like a loud banging, popping water balloon.
It tastes like a squidgy tomato sandwich.
It smells like hot smelling sick.
It feels like a bed of nails.
Reminds me of screaming down the stairs to my mum.

**Olivia Felton  (9)**
**Nutfield Church CE Primary School**


# Laughter

Laughter is a blue that is the colour of the clear sky.
Laughter tastes like a sausage that has just been cooked.
Laughter smells like the fresh smell of a river in the sun.
Laughter sounds like the waves crashing against the rocks.
Laughter reminds me of a soft pillow.

**Barnaby Yeldham  (10)**
**Nutfield Church CE Primary School**


# Fear

Fear is purple like smooth, dark velvet.
It sounds like warm, heavy breathing on the back of your neck.
Cold, hard granite is fear, smelling like rough, musty air.
It tastes like sharp, bitter lemon.
Fear reminds you of bleak, frosty fields.

**Ted Winder  (9)**
**Nutfield Church CE Primary School**

# Chips! Chips!

Chips! Chips!
You're wonderful stuff,
I love you, chips,
I can't get enough.
You're covered in salt
And you add the fish.
Chips! Chips!
You make a wonderful dish.

Chips! Chips!
You're really divine,
When I eat you,
You make me shine.
You're chewy and crunchy,
You're greasy and great.
Chips! Chips!
I want more on my plate.

Chips! Chips!
I love you a lot
You're my favourite,
Delicious and hot.
I gobble you down,
I just can't get enough.
Chips! Chips!
You're wonderful stuff.

**Charlie Dowden (9)**
**Nutfield Church CE Primary School**


# Hunger

Hunger is the colour brown because it reminds me of chocolate.
It sounds like popcorn being crunched by big teeth.
It smells like a banquet of food waiting for you to come.
It feels like a squidgy banana split.
It reminds me of a shop full of sweets and chocolate.

**Jack Mighall (9)**
**Nutfield Church CE Primary School**

# Autumn

Autumn is the time of year
When all the leaves shed a tear,
Wind starts to blow and leaves fall off
People start to sneeze and cough
The rain starts to come down
So in the morning you need a dressing gown.

The trees sway like a dog's tail
And you can hear the wind give a loud wail,
You hear the leaves give a tremble
So in the evening you can have apple crumble,
The wind turns into a gale,
So it is hard for the postman to deliver his mail.

In the morning it is really chilly,
So in school you are really silly,
The mornings get all foggy,
So you can't see and get all soggy.

**Jack Bellars (10)**
**Nutfield Church CE Primary School**


# Autumn

Angry autumn bites your skin
Cold and harmful using wind
People huddle to keep warm
Talking about the months which dawn
Little leaves and big ones too
Flutter down wet with dew
Mornings misty, dull and dark
Treacherous paths run through the park
Swaying branches creak with pain
And as usual splashed with rain
Now as winter slowly comes
All is quiet, all is calm.

**Joel Kemp (10)**
**Nutfield Church CE Primary School**

# Autumn And Winter

Autumn is damp,
Autumn is cold.
Roast dinner is new,
Ice lollies are old.
It's misty and rainy,
It's stormy and wild.
That's how I remember it as a lively, little child.

The leaves are all rustling,
They crackle and crunch.
Now it's time to go home
And have some nice lunch.
There's candles and wine,
A table set for six
And the Christmas tree in the corner,
The baubles hanging from the twigs.

We've all finished up,
Our tummies are full.
Now let's go outside
And play with snowballs.
We put on our coats, our gloves, scarves and hats
And what a surprise, so has the *cat!*

**Maisy Wyer (10)**
**Nutfield Church CE Primary School**

# Black Sadness

Sadness is black like black, dark roses.
Sadness sounds like someone crying on a black, silent night.
Sadness tastes like liquorice burning on my tongue.
Sadness smells like fire burning in front of my eyes.
Sadness feels like a gravestone crumbling into tiny pieces.
Sadness reminds me of dying flowers and sick animals.

**Marnie McAdam (9)**
**Nutfield Church CE Primary School**

# Autumn Poem

In autumn time leaves fall to the ground
And in the air they swirl around.
The weather is misty, blustery, breezy,
Through the window comes a leaf all cold and wheezy.

The trees are swaying, side to side,
The poor little robin has to hide.
It's dark, dull, miserable and blustery,
The ground is slippery, cold and muddy.
The leaves are rustling on the floor
And one slips in underneath the door.

Now the wind is dying down,
It's time for winter to come around.
White, glistening snow is much better
Than leafy, cold and rainy weather.
The Christmas turkey is coming along
And autumn has to flee and run.

**Dominic Harvey (10)**
**Nutfield Church CE Primary School**


# The Day Has Come . . .

The day has come for green leaves to fall
Off the trees that are so tall.
The day has come for the trees to sway
While all the little children play.
The day has come for a wet storm
The children are cold, so wrap them up warm.
The day has come for dew on the grass
Like pure water in a glass.
The day has come for all kinds of leaves
To fall off all kinds of trees.
Crunch and crackle, my favourite sounds
Autumn is here, so look around!

**Katie Richardson (10)**
**Nutfield Church CE Primary School**

# Autumn Bird

Some days are wet and cold,
Some are warm and dry.
Either way I'm always there,
Flying in the sky.

I perch on the golden trees,
Beneath my feet are rustling leaves.
I look down, so much to see,
Children jumping in the leaves.

Golden flakes falling all around,
Swirling, chasing, then floating to the ground.
As I move on, I spread my wings
And swoop up through the sky.
I feel the cold run past me,
As I clash with the leaves passing by.

Then I reach the orchard,
The trees bow down to me.
I sit on the ground waiting,
For the apples to fall at my feet.

After I've had my just fresh feast,
I set off down the street
And squawk away at all the coats,
Hugging the people I meet.

Now I head off to the woods,
Find sticks to build my nest
It's the end of another crisp autumn day
So now it's time to rest.

**Evangeline Foster (10)**
**Nutfield Church CE Primary School**

# Autumn Has Come At Last

Every year there comes a season
And it's put there for a specific reason.
Guy Fawkes, harvest and Hallowe'en.
They're everybody's autumn dream
Autumn has come at last.

The trees sway slowly to and fro
And all the leaves seem to let go.
It spreads out like a witch's coat
Autumn has come at last.

When the trees move, they look quite broad,
Changing colour of their own accord.
As the dew spreads round the field
You think, *how can this be real?*
Autumn has come at last.

The beautiful trees,
The numbing knees,
The glistening grass,
How I wish this could last.

But then one day and most sudden of all,
Icicles start to appear on the wall
Now it is here, it has finally come
Winter's here and autumn's gone
Winter has come at last.

**Caitlin Fine  (10)**
**Nutfield Church CE Primary School**

## The Dog's Breakfast

'No homework again,
What happened this time James?'
'I was feeding my pets, Sir.'
'Pets you don't have any pets.'
'Yes I do, I have a dog, a big dog!
My dog ate my homework, Sir.'
'Your dog ate your homework, James!'
'I could bring my dog in, Sir
And he could tell you about my homework.'
'Bring a dog into school, are you mad?'
'Yes Sir, my aunt was mad,
I must have caught it from her!'
'I give up James,
Bring me your homework tomorrow
And no dog!'
*Yes!*

**Lily Donovan (9)**
**Nutfield Church CE Primary School**


## Best Friend

Pencil and rubber are best friends,
Fork and knife are best friends,
Scissors and glue are best friends
Classroom and student are best friends
Jaimie and me are best friends
Sky and cloud are best friends
Flowers and butterflies are best friends
Children and toys are best friends
School and teachers are best friends.

**Ye-Rin Park (9)**
**Park Hill School**

# World War II

I was a child,
I was alone,
Where was I going?
Because it's not home.

Hope to see you soon,
How long will you be gone?
See you Mum
See you Dad
See you old home.

But wait, what is this?
Hello countryside,
Hello new home,
Hello new shop,
At the end of the road.

Why am I here
Is it a school trip?
We don't normally go this far,
So why am I doing this?

Do they hate me?
Is it true?
*No!*
It can't be,
It must be World War II.

**Jack Onslow  (10)**
**Park Hill School**

# I Love To Run!

I love to run across the plains,
So get a good grip on my reins,
We'll go so fast, we'll almost fly
And watch the world go zooming by . . .

**Tabitha Wallace  (10)**
**Park Hill School**

# The French Trip

Lots of fun and lots to do,
The chateau is fun for me and you.
Delicious food for us to eat,
A tuck shop for a tasty treat.
On trips and outings we go somewhere,
Like schools and orchards and other places there.
The activities you have to do,
Include escalade and using a canoe.
The night before the talent show,
We ate lots of delicious escargots.
On the talent night we had to sing,
Do the Locomotion and dancing.
Thank you so much for all you have done,
I loved the French trip it was so much fun.

**Jessica Hafenrichter  (10)**
**Park Hill School**


# The Trip To France

We went to France,
Our French to advance,
We stayed at a house
Where there wasn't a mouse.
But pigs, geese and a horse,
Plus lots of rabbits of course.
We had a good time,
The adults drank wine.
Before we left France,
We did a nice dance.
I thought canoeing was the best -
I came home for a rest!

**Antonia Harrison  (10)**
**Park Hill School**

# Chateau De La Baudonniere

We went to a chateau in France,
We got to sing and dance,
I tried to climb a wall
And thought I was going to fall,
I finally got to the top,
It was then I decided to stop!
We also made some bread,
That tasted good we said,
You've never a moment spare,
Or even to redo your hair!
Wish you could have been there too!
There's always so much to do,
Down at the Chateau de la Baudonniere,
There's so much more I like to share.
Au revoir, au revoir, au revoir.

**Jaimie Freeman  (9)**
**Park Hill School**


# The French Trip

The French trip was fun
And had a lot of sun.
The activities were the best,
Better than the rest,
The escalade was fab
And the canoeing
We had to do a lot of moving.
As for the escargot
I had to go - slow.

**Antonia Adams  (9)**
**Park Hill School**

# The Chateau

The chateau was really cool,
I especially liked the French school,
I always had room in my tummy,
For some snails that were so yummy.
In the canoeing, I won the race,
You should have seen the expression on my face.
In the evening I felt a little sad,
But while we were playing I felt glad.
This French trip I'll remember it forever
Will I forget it? No, probably never.

**Rebecca Anker  (9)**
**Park Hill School**

# The French Trip

The trip to the chateaux is the best I've had
I like it, I like it, I like it like mad
For the things we do are all so grand
The canoeing, the archery, the climbing are fun.

The French we speak, the food we eat
The children at school were all so sweet
The market we went to was oh so pleasant
Oh how I wish I could go again.

**Ellie Nearchou  (11)**
**Park Hill School**

# A Crab Who Is Looking For A Friend

A tanka about a crab who is looking for a friend

A crab with a thought
Looking by, to see a friend
Where have they all gone?
Looked in the sand and the sea
Come out, don't play hide-and-seek.

**Soo Yeon Hwang  (10)**
**Park Hill School**

# Fly Away

Have you ever thought one special day,
That you just want to fly away?
Fly into the fading fog,
Make all the living creatures sob,
Soar through summer, winter, autumn and spring,
Soar over valley and sheep grazing,
When all the villagers look up they sigh
And the forests are whispering, 'Oh my.'
I'd go through freezing nights and scorching days,
Just to fly, fly away.

**Hannah Calascione (10)**
**Park Hill School**


# Oreos

When I come home from school,
My mouth starts to drool.
I looked in the cookie jar
And what did I see
A fresh Oreo cookie waiting for me.

It smells like chocolate
With a vanilla filling cream.
When I look at that cream,
I start to dream.

It tastes delicious,
Scrumptious, delicious,
I like to eat as many as I can,
Especially when I'm sitting in the sand.

**Charlie Neuner (9)**
**Parkside School**

# Fiji

I like Fiji
As hot as the sun
It is my favourite country
Lying in the sun
I like the tropical fruit
In the bar
On top it has a star.

I like Fijians
I think they're cool
On the tree trunk
The monkeys are drunk.

I like Fiji
The sea is so clear
Dolphins and fish
Can be viewed from the pier.

I like Fiji
I could live there all my life
The scenery is beautiful
The plants
The flowers
The people too
It's a fantastic way to relax
I like Fiji.

**Ryan Baynes  (9)**
**Parkside School**


# Lazy Me

Sitting in my chair, looking at the screen
Thumbs working overtime, making footballer's kick
Left arrow, Spain win the ball
Hard down on the right arrow, England get the ball
Wish I was playing, not just my thumbs
Because I'd be Raul, so I could smack the ball.

**George Lewis  (9)**
**Parkside School**

# OJ Dragon Fury

Dragon, dragon, dragon stare,
Dragon, dragon, dragon flare,
Dragon, dragon in your lair,
Dragon, dragon, doesn't care.

'Dragon, did you eat an orang-utan?
Dragon, dragon, do you like your mustang?
Dragon what's that *clang, clang, clang?'*
Dragon's gonna give you a *bang, bang, bang!*

Dragon will you hit the spring fling?
Dragon please do your thing.
Dragon, dragon, you're the king,
Dragon says, 'Oh what the heck!
It's about time he took a rain check!

Dragon though it was a piece of cake
Gettin' the crowd startin' to shake.
Frankenstein saw his chance to take
As soon as he tried to play
The whole crowd started to quake
It's pretty obvious he was out of the fray.

**Hal Sherrington  (10)**
**Parkside School**


# Brazil

Brazil is my favourite country,
It has thousands of monkeys,
The monkeys swing,
The football fans sing.
The sun is bright,
Every day and night.
The statue in Rio is so tall,
It would make a dinosaur look small!
My friend Pedro lives in Brazil,
It's so hot you would frazzle!

**Ben Smith  (9)**
**Parkside School**

# So Furry

My rabbit was so furry
He was always in a hurry.
He used to make me worry
He was cuddly and snugly.

My rabbit was so furry
He was naughty and sporty.
Running when I wasn't looking
By the end of the race he was purring but I was panting.

My rabbit was so furry
His noises were all purry
He used to purr like a cat.

**Thomas Subba Row  (10)**
**Parkside School**


# Mischief Is . . .

A cute, cuddly, clumsy dog
As woolly as a bear
A sharp nip, a gnashing of teeth
In return for playful teasing.

Shaking a toy rabbit like a rag doll
Stealing biscuits from our plates
Crumbs around his mouth . . . the evidence
Attention seeker, a loveable rascal.

Come here! Put that down!
Don't do that! Don't chew my shoe!
That's my mischief,
That's my dog - Monty!

**Adam Jarvis  (10)**
**Parkside School**

# Jamaica

Jamaica is my favourite country
It smells of tropical monkey
Monkeys swing around the trees
And bash into all the leaves.

The men go round with long dreadlocks
They tuck them in a woollen box
A red, green and yellow hat
Upon some people's heads it sat.

Bob Marley's music is called reggae
In every bar I hear him play
As you eat your lovely lunch
Whilst drinking your beautiful rum punch.

The weather is so hot
Hot enough to boil a pot
The sea is sleek and smooth
All you can see is blue, blue, blue.

**Fraser Payne  (9)**
**Parkside School**


# The Romans

The Romans fight with all their might
Because they believe that might is right.
The Saxons were brave, but had no swords
The Romans were happy, especially the lords.

The gladiators fought for their lives
Because they wanted to get back to their lives.
The Romans lived in wonderful villas,
On both sides, such strong pillars.

Britain was conquered by the Romans
And made slaves out of all their bowman
But they were forced to return home
As the barbarians were attacking Rome.

**Robbie Heald  (10)**
**Parkside School**

# The Match Of The Day

It was the match of the day
Real Madrid versus AC Milan
Which team would have the final say
And who would be the happiest fan?

Roberto Carlos took a corner
The ball bobbed, bounced and landed in the area
Zidane was there to blast it in
1-0 to us! We're going to win.

Sherchenko, their top goal scorer, had the ball
But could he do it for them?
Salgado, as ferocious as a lion tackled him.
He flipped and fell face down

Free-kick to them just outside the box
It was their last chance to score a goal
The striker strode speedily to make the most
But luckily thumped it against the post!

**Matthew Callaway (10)**
**Parkside School**


# My Fish

My two fish, they live in a bowl
One's gold and the other is as black as coal.

The first is named Woody, the other is Buzz
They swim in the night like a little piece of fuzz.

They look at me because they want to eat
So then I give in and surprise them with a big, tasty treat.

The only thing annoying about my fish
Is when I have to clean out their stinky, smelly dish.

**Michael Neuner (11)**
**Parkside School**

# Chelsea Crazy

On a warm July evening in 2000
I sat in the changing room,
Listening to the *boom, boom, boom*
Of a million eager fans.
It was the FA Cup Final
Chelsea vs Arsenal
As we emerged from the tunnel
The whole of Cardiff roared raucously.
I was a player, a perfect player,
A player with perfect pace called Zola!
Right from the first kick they picked on me,
I was brought down in the penalty box.
My penalty kick was a little flick
Which just happened to nick the crossbar.
So I ran in and sorted things out!
There was a stupendous shout from the crowd.
We had won! We had won! We had won, won, *won!*

**Thomas Hilton-Stevens (10)**
Parkside School


# Spring

Spring is the season when the flowers come out,
The daffodils are everywhere,
The tulips and crocuses are bringing colours all over the garden
And all the birds are flying around and singing happy songs.

Spring is the season when
You can go outside and play
Football, hockey, cricket,
Swimming and unfortunately cross country.

The sun is getting higher in the sky
The air is getting warmer and all the young are born.

**Augustin Wauters (9)**
Parkside School

# A Mouse, A Louse And A Cat

There was a mouse
That lived in a house
It didn't like cats
That chase rats.
It had a spouse
That had a louse
With a little hat.
The louse was adventurous
And jumped on the cat
But lost its hat
And this was very bad.
The mouse saw the hat
Thought it was the louse
And came out to investigate
But the cat was ravenous
And the mouse she ate.

**Nicholas Kleiber  (9)**
**Parkside School**


# Why Did I Write This Poem?

Who invented homework,
Who invented school,
Who was the first teacher,
Why did they bother at all?

English and all its poems
Maths and all its sums
Science and Bunsen burner
Although history can be fun.

Poems are always the worst
It's hard to find a rhyme
I ponder for hours and hours
I think it's a waste of time.

**James Gair  (9)**
**Parkside School**

# A Dark Wood At Midnight

A dark wood at midnight, all is still,
The howl of the wind, the rustle of the leaves on the trees.
A twig snaps and footsteps echo in my mind.
I'm petrified and poor, ashamed of what I am.
I reach a place protected by the trees.
Someone has been here, a twig house is set.
It's not the best place, but it will do for a sec.
I crawl inside, an unsuspecting tramp,
But before I can think,
A hand grabs me by the scruff of the neck
And next thing I know
I'm out in the black,
A terrified tramp once more.
The haunting hoot of an owl.
The scratchy squeak of a rat.
The roaring clap of thunder
And I'm out in the wild once more.

**Christopher Yeates  (11)**
**Parkside School**


# My Dogs And Cats

My cats and dogs chase the frogs
All around the garden.
The cats eat the dogs' food
While the dogs eat the trash.
The cats chase the frogs,
While the dogs chase one another's tails
While the dogs fight
The cats watch with delight
The dogs are on diets
While the cats are happy and fat.

**Josh Gill  (11)**
**Parkside School**

# Moody Mountains

Snow-capped peaks glistening white
Sun reflected, dazzling bright,
Blue sky impossible to describe,
Breathe in the air and feel alive.

*Moody mountains*

Dark clouds shroud the peaks,
Dropping snow like great white sheets,
Blizzards make it impossible to see,
The silence deafening in its intensity.

*Moody mountains*

Lights of snowploughs cast an eerie glow,
Making tracks in the field of snow,
Like combine harvesters working the land,
So their winter cousins look just as grand.

*Moody mountains.*

**Toby Webb  (10)**
**Parkside School**


# TV

TV is heaven, could not live without it
If there was a power cut
I would have to get off my butt.

Some TV is funny
Some films contain ants
Some TV is so scary that they make you wet your pants.

If we did not have a TV
What would you do?
I would play some football as my brother shouts, 'Boo hoo!'

**Joshua Kingsley  (9)**
**Parkside School**

# My Favourite Place

Cornwall is the place to be,
Over the sun and over the sea.
Rocks and caves are fun to find,
Never stop until teatime.
Weather is the best of all,
Always sunny, it never pours.

Body boarding in the sea,
Twenty-four hours, enough for me
Then we get out to get dry
And get our sausages to fry.
We enjoy the lovely view
Bet you wish you could see it too.
Then we get ready for our bed
Lying down to rest our head.

Lovely fun with all my friends,
Lasting till the summer ends.

**Adam Laverick (10)**
**Parkside School**


# My Team

Our goalie is amazing, he never lets anything in,
That's why we normally win,
But our defenders are appalling, they let everything through,
That is why we drew with Crewe,
But our midfield sorts things out,
That's why they're always running about,
Our strikers are good,
But they always hit wood,
We are fit, we have fun and we're always on form!

**William Straughan (10)**
**Parkside School**

# My Not Pets

I have an elephant called Bill
A dolphin called Jill
A hippo called Phil
And a monkey called Dill.

A snake called Sam
A whale called Dan
An owl called Pam
And an antelope called Cam.

A dog called Matt
A cat called Zack
A pig called Jack
And a fish called Nat.

A panther called Larry,
A lion called Harry
A leopard called Sammy
And a tiger called Barry.

A swan called Seb
A worm called Greg
A snail called Ted
And a slug called Ned.

A horse called Zara
A cow called Kiara
A moose called Karla
And a butterfly called Breanna.

Oh . . . wait . . . no I don't!

**Adam Cannings (10)**
**Parkside School**

# The Field

In the countryside,
There is a wind, like no wind
Among the golden corn.

The tree's leaves
Fall as light as feathers
Onto the silky lawn.

The river's waters
Flow still and calmly
Between the river banks.

The heaven's clouds
Fly across the sky,
Like magical, flying carpets.

**Edward Stokes  (10)**
**Parkside School**


# The Silent Hunter

It sits by the side of a lake
With the patience of a snake
The heron sits there
Waiting, waiting, waiting
And when a fish is in sight
He pulls back his head . . .
And takes a ferocious bite!
And then the fish is gone
And so is the heron.
With wings outstretched,
The heron soars off into the skies
Piercing the bright, white clouds.

**Thomas Payne  (10)**
**Parkside School**

# The Monster Who Wanted To Be Friendly

There was a monster
A scary monster
Which nobody liked
He had a face
A scary face
Which nobody wanted to see
His face was as ugly as a rhino
But . . . inside, his heart was true and kind.

One day the monster
Went into town
He wanted to have a good look around
The people saw him, the children screamed
But . . . inside, there was a feeling his heart was still true and kind.

**Josh Howe  (10)**
**Parkside School**


# What Is Your Favourite Thing?

What is your favourite thing?
Is it family?
Well I suppose it should be
But what about chocolate?
The thing you can go to when no one else wants you,
Or what about television?
You sit in front of it and never get bored,
With your beady, little eyes staring at it,
For three hours straight.
Is your favourite thing books?
Or maybe poetry?
But I don't know what *your* favourite thing is
But mine is . . .

**William Boocock  (10)**
**Parkside School**

# An African Day Of Sound

I wake up in the morning hearing the birds sing sweet songs
I have breakfast listening to my cat
Scurrying, shouting around the garden
I trudge to school entranced by the sound
Of the wind singing, sailing, spilling its song
I work at school inspired by the noises
Of the snakes hissing, the lions roaring, the monkeys howling
And the frogs croaking.
When I go to sleep
All I can hear is a peace, a deafening silence
I go to sleep waiting for the song to begin again
I can't wait.

**Tim Maddin  (10)**
**Parkside School**


# Life As A Snail

Mr Snail, why are you so slow?
You are as slow as my mum driving.
What is that slime you produce?
It has covered my garden.
Is your shell annoying, dragging it around with you?
What is your purpose in life?

Mr Human, I am so slow because I like to take my time,
For I do not have a job to do.
The slime I produce is my trail for others to follow.
No, my shell is not annoying because it is my home.
I do not really have a purpose in life.

**Daniel Ferree  (10)**
**Parkside School**

# Spain

Spain is everyone's dream,
In the sky the sun shines and gleams,
The sky is bright blue
The football's for you
The birds fly free
The swimming pool's for me
Rub in your lotion
We're off to the beach
The sunset's a reddish-orange peach,
It's time to go home
Call Gran on her phone
What's that there?
It's our home.

**Edward Kennedy  (10)**
**Parkside School**


# Mr Tiggy

My cat is fat
He bounces after rats
He is a bouncy cat.

My cat is called Tigger
He is bigger than a dog
He can bounce higher than a frog.

My cat likes to dance
Like a monkey in France . . .
So let's get jiggy
With Mr Tiggy.

**Michael Isle  (10)**
**Parkside School**

# Football Crazy

I put on my shirt,
Number twenty-nine
I am playing
In the attacking line.

I passed to my friend
So good he is frightening
He is as fast
As greased lightning.

He passed me the ball
I was taken out
That got the crowd
Starting to shout.

I took one more shot
Then the final whistle blew
The ball was in the back of the net
I shouted, 'Phew!'

We'd won the game
1-0 was the score
The crowd on their feet
All screaming for more.

**Harry Dear (10)**
**Parkside School**


# Fish Tank

Fish tank,
I really like it,
Shh, you won't tell anyone - it's my wish tank.
The wish tank, grants any wish,
Not like a normal fish tank
And when you wish, you get it,
Not when you wish for a wish tank though,
Really wish you had a wish tank don't you?

**Stuart Mould (9)**
**Parkside School**

# The Witch's Cat . . .

Is very sleek, but her mind is bleak
The witch's cat is very fat,
She's always chasing the local rat.
The cat's bait could resign to the rat's fate.
The mousetrap goes, 'Ow! My nose.'
'Hooray,' says the cat, 'take that you pesky rat.'
She killed the rat
And shared it with her good friend the bat,
Who was equally callous.

**Jonathan Perkins  (10)**
**Parkside School**


# I'm Amazing

I'm amazing at rollerblading
I fly so high, over the birds in the sky.
When I come down I hit the floor
Bash my nose and it's really sore.

I'm amazing at cycling
I go so fast, over the treetops and through the dust.
When I come down I hit the floor
Broke my arm this time, now that's really sore.

**Nathan Crabtree  (11)**
**Parkside School**


# I'm Scared

I'm scared of bees in flight,
As well as the way trees sway at night.
I'm scared of bats,
But not pet cats.
I'm scared of sharks
And a big dog's bark.
But I will tell you what really makes you pray
Our teacher on a bad day.

**Ronnie Bowerman  (9)**
**Parkside School**

# Listen

Silence is . . .

The shine of light as it flicks on;
The drift of an iceberg gently floating;
The buzz of a battery working a toy;
The colour of flowing rainbows in the sky;
The orbit of planets slowly drifting;
The whisper of clouds lazily moving;
The zoom of gravity pulling down;
The swiftness of an eagle gracefully gliding;
The clank of bones wobbling inside us;
The flash of a camera as it comes to our eyes;
The scratch of a cat as it cuts into mice;
The communication of ants and wasps;
The chorus of silence has now come to Earth;
The chorus of silence has now come to Earth.

**William Franks  (10)**
**Reigate Priory School**


# In God's Hands The Lord Kept . . .

Ten yummy, wormy pieces of pasta
Nine big, fat, juicy potatoes,
Eight refreshing peaches
Seven packets of crunchy crisps
Six prickly pineapples
Five hard coconuts, hard and milky
Four crumbly crumbles
Three hot pies
Two loaves of white bread
And one lake of water.

**Sophie Mamalis  (8)**
**Reigate Priory School**

# The Daily Life Of A Farmer In Africa

I wake up
I put my clothes on
I sigh
I hope the crops . . .
Oh no! Water, water everywhere
Must have been a flood overnight
I go out and start work
I start cutting the crops with my sickle
It's lunchtime,
A leg of antelope and an empty shell full of water
Hottest part of the day
I sweat more than ever
Morning reveals a sorrowful sight
A swarm of insects are hovering over my crops.

**Athavan Bosch (8)**
Reigate Priory School


# God's Saved Us

In God's hands He kept for us . . .
Ten little white packs of rice,
Nine beans fresh from the field,
Eight swirly, coloured pieces of pasta,
Seven spoonfuls of strawberry yoghurt,
Six slices of white, soft bread,
Five boxes of different, nourishing breakfast cereals,
Four bright yellow, big bananas,
Three green, juicy apples,
Two tangerine oranges
And one million, guess what?
People!

**Beth Alderman (8)**
Reigate Priory School

# The Things We All Forget

We never think before eating,
Like how it was made or where it's been,
At harvest the farmers cut all the crops,
When they're in desperation and no one has seen.

A farmer in the morning,
Is a famous farmer soon,
A small cottage: one wife, one child
And working in the glistening moon.

You're trying to take a break
And trying to make a stop,
A spot of TV,
But the rain is making you drop.

You wake again next morning,
To hear the cries of your wife in despair,
You rush into your field
And none of the crops are there.

**Polly Griffiths (8)**
**Reigate Priory School**


# Thanking God

Ten grains of rice that go rolling off the table
Nine pasta shapes that twist and twirl
Eight pieces of ham that slip and slide
Seven black pieces of beef that sizzle
Six burger buns that snap and crackle
Five pancakes that turn and toss in the air
Four Scotch eggs that never stop crumbling
Three chicken wings that are burnt on top
Two chocolate cakes that are really delicious
And one, guess what?
My loveable God.

**Max Anderson (8)**
**Reigate Priory School**

# The Life Of A Poor Farmer

So I got the job
I don't know why
I sit gazing at the sky
Thinking about the wealthy countries
With lots of machinery
I get up at 5am after my sleep
It's another day hard at work
I get given an uncomfortable straw hat
A basket and a pair of filthy gloves
This is the worst season of the year
But it's not just at harvest time
I have to milk the cows all year through
Again, not like the wealthy countries with machinery
I have no machinery, only my hands.

**Lucy Pullinger (9)**
**Reigate Priory School**


# Harvest

Thank you God for . . .
Ten grains of tiny rice popping in the microwave
Nine bits of sweetcorn, yellow like the sun
Eight bits of slimy pasta cooking in a pan
Seven fat potatoes sizzling while they boil
Six big chocolate cookies rattling in the packet
Five pieces of cake all crumbly and brown
Four pieces of light brown slimy chicken
Three whole, crunchy orange carrots
Two fat green cabbages growing in my garden
And one of me!

**Beth Craske (8)**
**Reigate Priory School**

# Family

In my family there is my mother,
my father, my brother and me.

My mum is soon to be the smallest in the family,
the only one with green eyes and a great personality.

My dad is a wacky, super fun man, on goes the list,
even though he's a psychiatrist.

I have a brother, who's around the height of Big Ben,
only kidding, he's thirteen and five foot ten!

Then there's me, there's not much to say,
only that I love chilling out with my friends,
setting new trends, stroking my cat.

Then we have two cute cats who are very fat and as black as night,
their names are Misty and Highbury
and can miaow very loud and give a fright.

In my family there is my mother,
my father, my brother and me.

**Soracha Healy (10)**
**St Agatha's Catholic Primary School, Kingston-upon-Thames**

## Maybe It's Because I'm A Dowsett!

Maybe it's because I'm a Dowsett,
that I think my family is great.
But my mum thinks we're untidy,
I tell her it's a family trait.
We all love sport and it gets busy,
that is how I made such good mates.
We spend too long on the phone with them,
and that is exactly what my mum hates.
Our house is hectic in the morning,
no wonder we're often late.
Do we take too long in the bath,
or is it just the Dowsett's fate.

**Sophie Dowsett (10)**
**St Agatha's Catholic Primary School, Kingston-upon-Thames**

# Autumn

Leaves scatter on the ground,
crispy and golden brown.
Wild animals hibernate,
ducks and geese migrate.

Kicking multicoloured leaves,
in the Richmond Park,
in the navy skies,
very, very dark.

Soon it will be Hallowe'en,
trick or treat all night;
vampires in the bushes,
giving me a fright!

Fireworks shooting in the skies,
scaring all the butterflies,
but unfortunately,
the butterflies all die!

**Conor McGovern-Paul  (8)**
**St Agatha's Catholic Primary School, Kingston-upon-Thames**


# My Autumn Poem

It's autumn today hip, hip hooray,
And Hallowe'en is near,
Time to scare the life out of people.
The children playing in the garden, not for long,
Then it will go dark.

The poor leaves die, some stay green,
Because they are evergreens.
The days get shorter so I have to sleep in bed with Ted.
It's not fair, we get shorter days.

Now please leave me alone,
It's time for me to scare my family.
*Ha, ha, ha!*

**Vanessa Adofo  (8)**
**St Agatha's Catholic Primary School, Kingston-upon-Thames**

# When Autumn Comes In

When autumn comes in,
all those flowers begin,
to start drooping down to the ground,
without making a single sound!

When autumn comes in,
all those leaves begin,
to turn a different colour to that crispy brown!

When autumn comes in,
all those showers begin,
to make that blustery wind!

When autumn comes in,
Hallowe'en starts to loom,
all those ghosts hide in the gloom,
so don't get trapped in their doom!

When autumn comes in,
all the apples become ripe, with light,
I eat them in one big bite!

That's when autumn comes in.

**Christina Paish (8)**
**St Agatha's Catholic Primary School, Kingston-upon-Thames**

# Autumn

Children picking conkers off the ground without a sound.
Children playing in the park not for long, it's nearly dark.
The animals are hibernating in the trees.
Kicking and jumping in a bundle of leaves.

The plants are dying, trees are bare,
I feel like cuddling up with my teddy bear.

**Eleanor O'Leary (8)**
**St Agatha's Catholic Primary School, Kingston-upon-Thames**

# My Family

There are four people in my family,
My dad, my mum, my sister and me.
My dad is really fun and kind,
And I think of him as a busy bee.
My mum is short and tidy,
And can get in a muddle,
She is caring and helpful
And is brilliant to cuddle.
My sister is loving and pretty
And always thinks of others,
She wakes up early on weekdays,
But on weekends she stays under her covers.
There are four people in my family,
But I do have a canine pet,
He's black and white and scruffy,
And smells, especially when wet.
There are four people in my family,
My dad, my mum, my sister and me,
I think they're the best family,
And I love them all equally.

**Natalia Jezierski (10)**
St Agatha's Catholic Primary School, Kingston-upon-Thames

# Autumn

The skies are all misty,
leaves are on the ground,
running all around.

Kicking leaves in the park,
nights are very dark,
the trees are nearly bare,
Hallowe'en is coming soon,
I'm getting scared.

I'm all warm in my bed,
snuggling in with my ted.

**Josef James (8)**
St Agatha's Catholic Primary School, Kingston-upon-Thames

# Autumn Times

Gusts of wind everywhere,
helicopters spinning in the air.

Leaves scattered everywhere,
children playing in the park
not for long, it's almost dark.

I love autumn, I love autumn,
conkers rolling everywhere.

Animals hide, flowers die,
frostbite everywhere.

Autumn, such a scream,
pumpkins, vampires, ghosts, monsters,
very fun, it's dress up time!

Lots and lots and lots of fun!

**Luke Pearce  (8)**
**St Agatha's Catholic Primary School, Kingston-upon-Thames**


# My Autumn Poem

It's autumn today
Hip hip hooray
Time to go out and play.

It's Hallowe'en at last
Time's speeding very fast
It's time to be scared
But a time we can all share.

Apples are ripe
Falling from the trees
Not even waking the bees.

There's less daylight
And the mornings are not bright
It's even now midnight.

**Caitlin King  (8)**
**St Agatha's Catholic Primary School, Kingston-upon-Thames**

# Autumn Poem

Autumn is starting to rise,
Summer is saying its goodbyes,
Leaves are falling to the ground,
Children are kicking them all around.

Autumn is the time of year,
When the trees get bare,
The leaves change colours, red, yellow and brown,
As they seem to fly out of town.

The days get shorter and darker
As the animals hibernate in the park,
Squirrels hunting for acorns and nuts,
To hide away in their hut.

Hallowe'en is a time when we can go trick or treating
Suddenly you find candy at your feet.

The pumpkins are lit in the dark gloom,
The witches come out to ride on their broom.
The temperatures drop
As the flowers flop.

**Danielle Hernandez (8)**
**St Agatha's Catholic Primary School, Kingston-upon-Thames**


# My Autumn Poem

It's autumn today, hip hip hooray,
It's time to go out and enjoy our play
Leaves are crunchy all around
Making a very noisy sound.

It's Hallowe'en at last
And time to run very fast
Time to be scared
But a time when we can all share.

The leaves are all red
So that means it is time . . .
To go to bed!

**Daniela Cavallino (8)**
**St Agatha's Catholic Primary School, Kingston-upon-Thames**

# Autumn Poem

Leaves falling from the trees,
Making a big pile,
Today, the day when you come to play,
You could have a leaf fight.

It is Hallowe'en soon,
A scary time,
Yummy sweets,
Lots of masks to design.

Golden yellow,
Red and brown,
Rain makes water,
So don't drown.

Birds have gone,
They have flown away,
Come on sun, you're number one,
We need you here today.

The crunchy leaves make a sound
But they only crunch, when you touch the ground.

**Amber Kijowski (8)**
**St Agatha's Catholic Primary School, Kingston-upon-Thames**


# Autumn

A gust of wind in my face
Boys playing football down my place.
One hundred leaves on the road
A crunchy noise on the golden land.

As the nights grow longer and the days grow shorter
The sun has to change its way.
Frostbite in the morning and frostbite at night,
It's never changing its way.

Conkers are broken in the park,
Friends laugh till it's dark.

**Fiona Kitchen (8)**
**St Agatha's Catholic Primary School, Kingston-upon-Thames**

# Fear

Fear is blue, like the shadowed night sky,
It sounds like the terror of a wailing infant,
It tastes like a shadow, darting along the ground,
It smells like a need for company, a thirst, a want,
It looks like a pale shiver running up me,
It feels like a sad, cold sheet covering my heart,
It reminds me of a wolf in the shadow that you can't see.

**Dasha Barsky (10)**
St John's Primary School, Woking

# Laughter

Laughter is orange like sunshine.
Laughter sounds like singing.
Laughter tastes like mouth-watering chocolates.
Laughter smells like red roses.
Laughter feels like silk cloth.
Laughter reminds me of my friends.

**Elizabeth Westmacott (9)**
St John's Primary School, Woking

# Anger

Anger is as red as fire,
Anger sounds like an explosion,
Anger tastes like blood,
Anger smells like trouble,
Anger feels like a pin pushed in your arm,
Anger reminds me of hate.

**Cameron Purdie (9)**
St John's Primary School, Woking

# Hate

Hate is black, black like murder.
Hate is someone taking out their anger.
Hate is a drum, pounding in your head.
Hate is pain, destroying your insides.
Hate is danger, making you out of control.
Hate is blood, blood coming up your mouth.
Hate is being left-out, making you feel that you're not wanted.
Hate is a feeling I would not want to have.

**Jake Powell  (10)**
St John's Primary School, Woking


# Love

Love is red like a heart,
Love sounds like a heartbeat,
Love tastes like yummy sweets,
Love smells like roses,
Love feels like soft flowers,
Love reminds me of my mum and dad.

**Jennifer Atkinson  (9)**
St John's Primary School, Woking


# Fun

Fun is red with yellow polka dots,
Fun sounds like people going mental,
Fun tastes like chocolate sponge cake,
Fun smells like freshly made bread,
Fun feels like cuddly toys,
Fun reminds me of my mummy.

**Billy Hack  (9)**
St John's Primary School, Woking

# Silence

Silence is white like a blank piece of paper
Silence feels like a gentle touch on my shoulder
Silence looks like a dove with an olive branch in his beak
Silence sounds like nothing, no one's there
Silence tastes like plain food being eaten
Silence smells like marshmallows, melting on the fire
Silence reminds me of a unicorn flying high.

**Megan Oakley (10)**
St John's Primary School, Woking


# Fun

Fun is yellow with pink polka dots all over.
Fun sounds happy like the laughter of a little girl.
Fun tastes like your favourite food or pudding.
Fun smells like flowers with pollen.
Fun feels like a teddy bear you've always loved.
Fun reminds me of happy memories.

**Josie Pullen (9)**
St John's Primary School, Woking


# Anger

Anger is the colour of a bubbling, boiling lava pool.
Anger sounds like thunder and lightning.
Anger tastes like blood.
Anger smells like trouble.
Anger feels like madness.
Anger reminds me of red.

**Georgia Compton (9)**
St John's Primary School, Woking

# Laughter

Laughter is orange.
Laughter tastes like a roast on Christmas Day.
Laughter sounds loud.
Laughter reminds me of when I am on holiday.
Laughter looks like a smile.
Laughter smells like a piece of fresh cake.
Laughter feels fun.

**Stephen Nicholls (10)**
St John's Primary School, Woking

# Happiness Is . . .

Happiness is yellow, like daffodils in the summer breeze.
Happiness sounds like people laughing.
Happiness smells like a ripe banana which has just been peeled.
Happiness is lots of happy children smiling.
Happiness feels like a big hug.
Happiness tastes like vanilla ice cream.
Happiness reminds me of people having a good time.

**Katie Jane Taggart (10)**
St John's Primary School, Woking

# Happiness

It is gold to brighten things up.
It looks like a swan swimming in peace.
It smells like Grandma cooking Christmas pudding.
It sounds like a choir of blue tits in the tree.
It feels like a present from God.
It tastes like a toffee apple for desert.
It reminds me of a gift of light.

**Michael Gent (10)**
St John's Primary School, Woking

# Laughter

Laughter is yellow, like the sunshine
It sounds like birds singing in the summer sun
It smells like marshmallows, roasting on a fire
It tastes like sweet, mellow fruits
It feels like a calm river flowing through my body
It looks like a small baby bunny
It reminds me of the sunny summer.

**Chloe Walker  (10)**
**St John's Primary School, Woking**


# Fireworks

On a cold autumn night
The fireworks shine so bright
The bonfire is so high
It lights up the sky.

The rockets shoot into the sky
The sparklers fizz until they die
The Catherine wheels begin to spin
Then Mum says, 'I hope the cat's in.'

Toasting marshmallows on the fire
Is just my heart's desire
My hands are cold
My nose is runny
I wish the weather was sunny.

As the fire begins to die
All the children start to cry
'It's time for bed,' Daddy said
'Where's my ted?'
'Get into bed!'
But my brother said, 'But these pyjamas are red!'

**Rebecca Parker  (8)**
**St Martin's Junior School, Epsom**

# Timmy The Bear

My little bear, his name is Timmy
He lives in my house with a dog called Jimmy
At night he sleeps on my bed
Just by my pillow next to my head
He's got a skateboard and some shades
I'm going to get him some shiny new blades
I got Timmy from Croydon Town
Could have got a rabbit or a clown
He's my best friend, Timmy the bear
He's got pink and red, short, spiky hair
I put his little coat on and take him to school
He shouldn't go really, not as a rule
He waits in my bag while I play with my friends
And at the end of the day he comes home again
I love little Timmy, he's cuddly and nice
I think he'll be with me the rest of my life.

**Jodie Battershell (9)**
**St Martin's Junior School, Epsom**


# Four Seasons

A blanket of snow will start the year,
With crystals of ice scattered everywhere.
Spring comes round with tulip and rose,
Then wash them all down with the cold water hose.
Summer will come with temperatures rising,
Scented jasmine and honeysuckle thriving.
Autumn brings dry, crispy leaves,
Helped to fall by a cold, blowy breeze.
A blanket of snow will end the year,
With crystals of ice scattered everywhere.

**John Vagg (10)**
**St Martin's Junior School, Epsom**

# Once Upon A Rhyme

Once upon a rhyme
In a very ancient time,

Long before our lives began
There lived a very ancient man.

Upon his face a story told
Of a once young man, brave and bold

And now his body lies down in the dirt
Where that brave young warrior was mortally hurt.

He died inside that pit of doom
Where snakes and lions will always loom

And now each year upon the hour
The sky will give a giant shower,

As if to say it missed him too
It missed the things he used to do.

And now this poem will end right here
Like a bullet ends the life of a deer.

**Allan Macleod  (10)**
**St Martin's Junior School, Epsom**


# What Is Blue?

What is blue? Jet stream is blue
As bright as a spring morning.

What is red? Fire is red
To burn for an eternity to come.

What is black? The abyss is black
The deep, dark, dangerous abyss.

What is orange? A fox is orange
A sleek, sly fox that lies in wait.

What is wonderful? The Earth is wonderful
The Earth with all its colours.

**Henry Glasford  (9)**
**St Martin's Junior School, Epsom**

# My Favourite Team

Arsenal, my favourite footy team,
They shoot, shoot, shoot and score
And when they win a match,
I dance around the floor.

I bet they'll win their next match,
I'll tell you about the dare,
The one who is the loser,
Has to eat a rotten pear.

They won their next match with Man U
And I won the bet,
But Arsenal were out of the league,
For arguing about a goal they didn't get.

It was so embarrassing,
I could die on a rack,
But you watch out Man U,
We'll soon be back.

**Ali Raja  (9)**
**St Martin's Junior School, Epsom**


# One Girl, Five Wonders

I lay in my bed and wondered why,
The colour blue is in the sky.
I looked out the window and saw the stars
And wondered why Earth isn't Mars.
I went to the park and to the swings
And wondered why we don't have wings.

I sat in my chair watching TV
And wondered how we came to be.
I wondered why, whilst eating toast,
We are so scared of ghosts.
I'll find the answer somehow, someday,
But for now they're locked up out of harm's way.

**Danielle Carvey  (10)**
**St Martin's Junior School, Epsom**

# St Martin's Is The Best

St Martin's is the best
All the children are nice
Everyone tries their best
And even the food is nice

The teachers are good
The parents also
The surroundings are good
The trips also

I'll be sad to go
Very soon Year 6 will finish
To schools all new, here we go
Our memories of St Martin's will not finish.

**Kieran Rose  (10)**
**St Martin's Junior School, Epsom**


# Have You Met My Pet Alien?

He lives in the shed
and sleeps on an air bed.

He has eight legs
and likes eating eggs.

His name is Dave
and he's really brave.

He's very smelly
and has a big belly.

He wears a red hat
and likes stroking the cat.

He has three big, blue eyes
and wears yellow ties.

**Katie Williams  (8)**
**St Martin's Junior School, Epsom**

# Mrs Daltry

Mrs Daltry is our teacher,
She's a nightmare to say the least,
She looks at young, tender children,
Then she'll have a feast.

Mrs Daltry is our teacher,
She looks daggers and knives,
Some children faint,
Others lose their lives.

Mrs Daltry is our teacher,
She's a horrible old witch,
She looks like an old hag,
She makes me feel as hollow as a ditch.

Mrs Daltry is our teacher,
You'd better watch out,
She's the most fearsome teacher to ever live,
She makes you want to put her head in a sieve.

Mrs Daltry is our teacher,
You can't deny it's true,
But there's nothing to fear now, she's not here,
Good heaven's, she's right behind you!

**Haissam Adil  (10)**
**St Martin's Junior School, Epsom**


# Soup

Monday's soup was very plain,
Tuesday's soup came from Spain,
Wednesday's soup was out of date,
Thursdays' soup came on a plate,
Friday's soup was thick like custard,
Saturday's soup tasted like mustard,
But the one that's eaten on the Sabbath day
Is very expensive so save up and pay!

**Jodie Rogers  (10)**
**St Martin's Junior School, Epsom**

# The Robin

I saw a robin redbreast
Up inside a tree,
It had three little babies,
Looking down at me.

Five or six months later,
Those babies learnt to fly,
One of them took off
And glided to the sky.

Another little robin,
Flew to the ground,
Picked out a wriggly worm,
Which wriggled round and round.

**Farah Faheem  (10)**
**St Martin's Junior School, Epsom**


# Under The Willow Tree

Under the willow tree
Where the branches hang low
The peaceful rustle
When the leaves blow.

In the house
By the grandfather clock
As the hands go round
There's a gentle tick-tock.

Outside in the rain
Where I'm getting soaked
Sodden patches
Where I've been poked . . .
Gently by the rain.

**Libby Woolgar  (9)**
**St Martin's Junior School, Epsom**

# She Glided Through The Darkness

She glided through the darkness
Looking for a friend.
She dipped and dived through the air
Wonders followed her closely.

Her gentle, warm feeling
Wrapped around my body.
She calmed and comforted me and you
Whispered us a song so strange.

I saw her in my window.
I saw her cold and loving face.
I saw her blue glittery, smiling lips.
I saw her silvery hair shine and glow.

She twinkled her starry eyebrows.
She brushed back her curls.
She looked at me mysteriously.
As she disappeared the window filled with sparks.

She bathed in the moonlit lake.
She climbed the shadowy tree.
She lay on the damp, icy rocks.
She scattered the morning dew.

She rushed through the dawn
Collecting the shimmering, fading stars.
She lost her glow and twinkly look.
She disappeared but tonight she'll come again.

**Anya Mooney (10)**
**Tatsfield Primary School**

# The Night I Thought A Thought

One night I fell asleep,
That night I had a dream,
All that night I thought a thought,
Did the dreamer fall asleep?

The treasurer holds keys to the dreams untold,
They wait for the dreamer to complete all the dreams,
And then dream all the dreams to the end,
They sail through your memory and keep you safe at night.

For one too many reasons I have a dream to tell.
All around a man was standing so quietly in a room,
Thinking of a story, a never-ending story,
For dreamers to tell through and through.

He had found a dream of small, small tales, swinging to and fro,
Everyone has their story; pirates, treasure and gold,
The dreamer will fly far from here just to have those dreams unfold,
While making a treasurer's dream my imagination was set free.

All around a ghost of pale white shades flickered back and forth,
Searching for a happiness like a delicate floating mist,
Dust dispersing and sinking through my tongue,
Made me wish to wake and run.

I started to see a light shining through a gap,
I started to open my eyes, I saw a flickering flame die out,
I shuffled around and put on some clothes, I started to think,
I sat and thought a thought, has the dreamer woken up yet?

**Reuben Aitken-Till (10)**
**Tatsfield Primary School**

# Little Bo Peep Was Asleep With All Her Sheep

Little Bo Peep was asleep, with all her sheep,
In the hay.
Then she heard, 'Run, run, I'm the gingerbread man.'
She woke up licking her lips.
'Run, run or I will eat you,' she said.
The gingerbread man stopped running.

When he saw Little Bo Peep, 'Oh you look pretty.'
'Oh you look tasty,' Little Bo Peep said craftily,
'Do you want to go for a walk in the wood?'
'OK,' said The gingerbread man.

While they were on their walk
The gingerbread man said, 'Do kiss me.'
'Yes please.'
While Little Bo Peep was kissing him
Little Bo Peep gobbled him up
Mmmmmmm!

**Katie Pratt (9)**
**Tatsfield Primary School**


# Little Bo Peep And The Gingerbread Man Poem

Little Bo Peep has locked herself out
She doesn't know what to do.
She is very tired and sleeps in the hay.

An hour later she is awakened from her dreams.
Suddenly she hears the sheep and wakes up
To find the gingerbread man on her favourite sheep.
'Get off my sheep, you will kill it!'

'Run, run, I am the gingerbread man.'
'Oh you look tasty.'
'Come here and I will tell you a secret.'
Gobble, gobble.
Gone, mmmmm.

**Daisy Richardson (9)**
**Tatsfield Primary School**

# The Night Queen

From her palace she flies towards the stars,
Higher into the atmosphere.
When finally she sees planet Mars,
Then she returns to us.

Her appearance is filled with beauty,
Her eyes beat like gold.
She is a queen of rich 'booty',
Her robes are like Christmas snow.

Her teeth are gleaming,
Her beauty is redeeming.
Her great smile's beaming,
At us in our night-time dreaming.

Before she goes, she looks back
At her sleeping subjects.
She flies up into the starry black,
And tomorrow she'll come again.

**Martin Barlow (10)**
**Tatsfield Primary School**


# The Boy

I saw a boy,
Who found a toy.
He played with it,
For a little bit.
He got bored
And went abroad.

On the plane,
He found it again.
He played with it
For a little bit,
It started to beep,
So he went to sleep.

**James Tetzner (10)**
**Tatsfield Primary School**

# Night!

I saw Night the other day,
I saw his evil face,
I heard him say, 'Hello my dear,'
In a devilish way.

His voice sounds like a blue bird,
His feet an elephant drum,
His voice made me shiver,
This is not real, this is absurd!

He smells so fresh,
It is like he has had a bath!
His perfume like countryside air,
So fresh it made me laugh.

He was dressed in safe black clothes,
With an oil lamp of clay,
He had a big golden sack,
And took all my bad dreams away.

I saw Night the other day,
I saw his evil face,
I heard him say, 'Goodbye my dear,'
In a devilish way.

**Chloe Shimmins (10)**
**Tatsfield Primary School**

# Dragon

I saw a dragon yesterday,
Its wings were large and spiky.
I saw a dragon yesterday,
Its body was really stripy.
His claws were really sharp.
His fire like an exploding bomb
And his name was Tommy Wiffin.
I saw a dragon yesterday,
Maybe you will too.

**Bethany Nairne (10)**
**Tatsfield Primary School**

# Little Bo Peep And Gingerbread Man Poem

Little Bo Peep was walking happily
Along with her sheep,
Then a gingerbread man came running along
With his beep.

'Where are you going in such a hurry?' she asked.
'I don't know but I know where you are going,' he said.
He went down the road quite thoughtfully,
'I am so magic aren't I?' said he.

'I am going to cast a spell on you,' he whispered.
'I wouldn't have it any other way,' she replied.
So he did it and she turned into a little gingerbread woman.
'Will you marry me now?' he asked.

The spell broke by the time the gingerbread man
Came back with all the rings and stuff.
Little Bo Peep was very hungry at that time
So she ate him of course.

**Rachel Dickens  (9)**
**Tatsfield Primary School**


# Monster

I saw a monster yesterday,
Its wooden jaws tried to grab me.
I saw a monster yesterday,
Its glowing eye made me flee.
His teeth were white and shiny
His fingers were made from traffic lights,
He was ready to eat you up.
I saw a monster yesterday,
Maybe you will too.

**Rhys Woodward  (10)**
**Tatsfield Primary School**

*Young Writers - Once Upon A Rhyme Poems From Surrey*

# Little Bo Peep And The Gingerbread Man Poem

Little Bo Peep was sleeping quietly
And she was leaning against the hay.
Maybe she had a bit too much food
At Little Boy Blue's birthday.

Meanwhile the gingerbread man
Had a treacherous plan.
Suddenly! Woke up Little Bo Peep
To hear galloping of her sheep.

'Thanks for returning my sheep,' she said.
He looked at her with a grin
Thoughts in his head of Bo Peep dead
Then he chased her for his dinner.

'Run Little Bo Peep, but I shall catch you.'
Crunch! Crunch! Crunch!
'That was tasty, yum, yum, yum!'
And that was the end of Little Bo Peep.

**Bridey Clifton (9)**
**Tatsfield Primary School**


# Dragon

I saw a dragon yesterday,
Its claws were as sharp as sharp can be.
I saw a dragon yesterday,
It was taller than you, on top of me.
His fiery breath was as hot as lava,
His tail was five feet long,
His scales were very spiky
And as hard as a piece of bamboo.
I saw a dragon yesterday,
Maybe you will too.

**Ben Harris (10)**
**Tatsfield Primary School**

## Little Bo Peep And Gingerbread Man Poem

Little Bo Peep was walking happily
Through the woods with her sheep.
She met the Gingerbread Man along the way
And said, 'What are you up to this week?'

The Gingerbread Man replied craftily
'I'm taking a walk in the woods.'
As they strolled along the path
He followed as close as he could.

She looked over her left shoulder
And she saw a bottle on the floor
And she saw a foot peeping out
When she started to walk to the foot, she fell over.

She landed in the poison
The Gingerbread Man shouted,
'Yes, she slipped in it!'
So he ran over to her sheep and he stole them.

**Jessica Salliss (9)**
**Tatsfield Primary School**


## I Saw A Monster In The Park

I saw a monster yesterday,
It was green and walked silently.
I saw a monster yesterday,
Its eyes were glowing brightly
And his teeth were dripping blood.
He was big and strong and fat,
He was hairy, scary and had a dragon tattoo,
If you see him maybe he'll go, 'Boo!'
I saw a monster yesterday,
Maybe you will too.

**Scott Mathews (10)**
**Tatsfield Primary School**

*Young Writers - Once Upon A Rhyme Poems From Surrey*

# The Night Charmer

She drifted through the moonlit sky,
Who is this strange lady?
She shuts the lids of the human eye,
What is this lady's name?

She lives by the river in a hut made of magical dreams,
She eats from the fruit trees
And drinks from the stream,
She feeds all the foxes and loves everyone,
She taunts all the nightmares and strikes the Devil dumb.

She floated over the still, cold pond,
Why does she clasp the nightmares?
She wandered, singing comforting songs,
Her spirit lingers within us.

In day she strikes her spell on nature,
In night she sends wishes to everyone,
She is the one who charms the sunset,
She is the queen of the night!

**Jay White  (10)**
**Tatsfield Primary School**


# I Saw A Dragon Yesterday

I saw a dragon yesterday
It was a very evil one,
I saw a dragon yesterday
It was basking in the sun,
His nose was blocked
His tail was spiky
And his front foot was as smelly
As a stinking skunk,
I saw a dragon yesterday
Maybe you will too.

**Jonathan Layton  (10)**
**Tatsfield Primary School**

# Night

I saw Night yesterday,
Night looks like a supermodel.
Her hair and lips are midnight-blue,
Clothes piled in a stack,
Her garb is like an astronaut's.

I saw Night yesterday,
Her voice sounds like a serenading bird.
Echoing feet like an elephant,
And her brother, Day, sounds like a shooting star.

I saw Night yesterday,
Her taste is like blooming violets
And like winter air.
The taste of her hair is lovely and fruity,
Her nails taste like sweet dreams.

I saw Night yesterday,
She smells like summer's flowers
And autumn leaves.
She can smell of bonfires lingering from Day.

I saw Night yesterday,
She feels like baby-soft skin,
Just been born.
Night feels scary but happy.
That's why she makes us warm at night.

**Emma Knights (10)**
**Tatsfield Primary School**

# Sweet Dreams

She is kind and comforting
And her colours fill the air
Her eyes are light and purple,
And they twinkle everywhere.

She fills my head with magical thoughts
Of fairy castles, a knight with a shining shield.
Her darkness is like velvet
Her moon is like a round cornfield.

The colours of night are dreamy,
Purple, blue and gold.
Her face smiles gently down on me,
As lovely dreams unfold.

While stars watch over me,
Like the grandma I never knew,
Night makes me warm and safe
Clad in a cloak of blue.

Night's hair is pink and flowing.
She glides across the sky,
Her scarlet robes move silently along,
She utters a gentle sigh.

Night breathes her sweet scent into the air
She touches everything that is asleep.
She brings starry dreams to all our minds
That stay forever in our thoughts to keep.

**Susannah Layton (10)**
**Tatsfield Primary School**

# Little Bo Peep And The Gingerbread Man Poem

*'Little Bo Peep had lost her sheep*
*And didn't know where to find them'*
She got punished by her dad,
He said she had to muck out the pigs on the farm.

But it happened to be that the gingerbread man
Was there too because he was walking along.
He was so tired he decided to have a sleep
In the chickens' cage because the chickens were out
But when he woke up . . .
He saw a girl crying,
She was trying to muck out the pigs on the farm.
At first the gingerbread man remembered
It was Little Bo Peep,
Then Little Bo Peep saw him and said,
'What on earth are you?'
The gingerbread man shouted back,
'What do you think I look like?'
'Sorry I know what you are, you're the gingerbread man,'
Little Bo Peep said quickly,
'And you certainly look tasty!'

The gingerbread man said, 'Thank you!'
And she said, 'I don't know why you're saying thank you.'
*Munch! Munch!*
*'Yummy, yummy in my tummy!'*

**Emma Sheehan  (9)**
**Tatsfield Primary School**

# Little Bo Peep And Gingerbread Man

Gingerbread man was having a morning jog,
When he needed a rest.
So he jogged into a farm
And thought the pig sties were the best.

Meanwhile a big, bad wolf
Was chasing Little Bo Peep and her sheep.
She finally left him behind
But ran to a set of pigsties,
Full of hay, knee-deep.

'My name is Gingerbread Man.
I hope you know you disturbed my sleep.'
'Oh, I'm sorry, I'm Little Bo Peep.
These are my sheep,' said Little Bo Peep.
'If you would like to have a peep?' asked Little Bo Peep.

'I've been chasing my sheep all day
And I haven't even had lunch,
I'll just have you,'
Dribbled Little Bo Peep
With a munch, a crunch, crack, a bite, a nibble and a chew.

All that was left of Gingerbread Man
Were his crumbs left in a bunch.

**Jim Blackman  (9)**
**Tatsfield Primary School**

# The Night Witch

Floating in the sunset breeze
I saw the night witch
Beneath the trees.

Her flowing hair was hanging down
She wore a light, silky gown.
She was neither evil nor kind.
She was a night witch
With a magical mind.

She wandered in the darkness of the forest
Full of magic and dreams.
There was no sound,
It was oh so quiet
Apart from the nearby stream.

The sky became lighter,
Everything was bright.
The night witch walked away,
'Sweet dreams,' she said,
'Goodnight!'

**Helen Gorringe  (10)**
**Tatsfield Primary School**


# Dragon

I saw a dragon yesterday,
Its spikes were flaming hot.
I saw a dragon yesterday,
A ferocious flame he shot.
His teeth were sharp,
His mouth was wide.

I saw him at the park at noon
So hopefully you will too,
But be careful,
His eyes maybe *set on you!*

**Emma Louise Pratt  (10)**
**Tatsfield Primary School**

# Night

Night is blood-curdling
Mad, nasty and lonesome.

Night will steal your dreams
And give you horrific nightmares.
He's a burglar,
Gliding through the dark sky.

He has a black fiery face,
Golden star eyes,
Dark blue wrinkly lips,
Purple shadowy hair.

His white, sparkling cloak twinkles
As he glides
Through departing day
And converts it into cheerless black sky.

He lives in the stars,
Leaving murky mist behind
As light comes back to life.

**Bradley Waite  (11)**
**Tatsfield Primary School**

# Dragon Poem

I saw a dragon yesterday,
Its wings were great and long.
I saw a dragon yesterday,
It was smelly and it did pong.
His tail was long and thick,
His breath would make you sick.
His eyes were big and blue,
I saw a dragon yesterday,
Maybe you will too.

**Matthew Benison  (10)**
**Tatsfield Primary School**

# Night-Time Calls

I won't go to sleep, I won't
I won't let Night grab me with his big black claws.
He has already taken the sun
I won't let him put me to sleep.

I know Night is lonely, but he is bold.
He is a thief, a crafty one,
A nasty, scary, senile one.
He is not young but neither old.

The planets are his features,
The stars are his eyes.
He moves around like a silver swan,
Across the moonlit skies.

He gives us presents every night -
Nightmares full of ghosts.
He is the man that lives in the moon.
Our sweet dreams, his hosts.

Inside his mouth a thousand stars,
Around his neck a big black cloak.
His glance becomes a lightning flash,
Like a thundercloud he spoke.

He left us all with darkness,
Stole the evening light.
Faded out the colours -
No blues, no greens, no white.

'Sleep tight my angel,' Mum's tone is soft
Her voice reassuring across the gloom.
I am cosy, warm and feeling loved,
For Mr Night the spell of doom.

**Esther Richmond  (10)**
**Tatsfield Primary School**

# Night

If Night were a figure
He would be scary.
The frightful dark skin
He is not like a fairy.

He steals your dreams
Replaces them with nightmares.
Moves through minds
But gets trapped in daylight.

Everything on him
Is dark as night.
Except for a tattoo
A white shiny star.

He sounds like a blackbird
Squawking at night.
He is transparent
And smells of rotten pike.

If Night were a figure
He would be scary.
His frightful dark skin
He is not like a fairy.

**Edward Irving  (10)**
**Tatsfield Primary School**

# Night

You come around every day,
Black coat draping across the sky,
Always this familiar way
Creeping slowly you pass by.

Smartly dressed your suit is black,
Charcoal-grey your tie,
Coat that swirls as you turn your back,
On your head a top hat so high.

Upon your shoulders your head like the moon,
Stars freckled around your face,
Your eyes shine like a silver spoon,
Every breath flows into space.

Gracefully you fade away,
The light surrounds your being,
At the dawn of a new day
Your visibility fleeing.

**Dominic Menham (10)**
**Tatsfield Primary School**


# Smelly Monster

I saw a monster yesterday
It smelt like rotten cheese.
I saw a monster yesterday
Its teeth were the colour of peas.
His body smelt like an old bomb,
His hat looked like a baseball bat.
I saw a monster yesterday
Maybe you will too.

**Charles Boys (10)**
**Tatsfield Primary School**

*Young Writers - Once Upon A Rhyme Poems From Surrey*

# Little Bo Peep And The Gingerbread Man

The gingerbread man
Ate too much ham
At Little Boy Blue's birthday
He ran, ran, ran and ate it more happily.

Little Bo Peep was running by
A pig sty.
She fell down, down
And ended up hearing a noise.

It was coming from a pig sty.
She fell over and died.
Oh poor Little Bo Peep.
Sorry folks but that's the end.

The gingerbread man was eaten up
And he went nuts.
When there was only one crumb left
A bear came and ate it instead.

**Samuel Minahan (9)**
**Tatsfield Primary School**


# The Prince Of Sleep

He is mystical and magical
Silent in his sleep.
As he creeps around the town
His whistle begins to peep.

His short blond hair
Blowing in the breeze.
With his moonlit face
He begins to sneeze.

Blowing his nightmares all over the town,
With his frightening fears
He whispers into people's ears
With his sparkly crown.

**Rosy Kingdon (10)**
**Tatsfield Primary School**

# The Playground Monster

It grabbed me with its tentacles,
It set a small tree alight,
It crushed a pair of spectacles,
It gave the teacher a fright.

Its green slime glued me to the ground,
Its smoky hair, smoked the air,
It drank a pond that it found,
Then it destroyed a funfair.

I did not know what to do,
It was eating up the school,
I was scared and I couldn't speak,
I looked very much like a fool.

It grabbed me with its tentacles,
It set a small tree alight,
Now don't give me those chuckles,
'Cause you might see him tonight.

**Ryan Reynolds  (11)**
**Tatsfield Primary School**


# Monster

I saw a monster yesterday,
Its head was like a duck.
I saw a monster yesterday,
Its legs were covered in muck.
His body was as long as a train,
His tail was as sharp as a cone.
I saw a monster yesterday,
Maybe you will too.

**Alex Holmes  (10)**
**Tatsfield Primary School**

## Little Bo Peep And Gingerbread Man Poem

The gingerbread man was running from the cook.
'Run, run, run as fast as you can, you can't catch me,
Because I'm the gingerbread man.'
The cook stopped.

Little Bo Peep was in the pig sty with her sheep.
The gingerbread man was running.
He met Little Bo Peep, so the gingerbread man
Helped Little Bo Peep with her sheep.

They went back to her house
And she got a picnic ready for the lake.
They then went to the lake with the sheep.
They sat down and had something to eat.

The gingerbread man got on Little Bo Peep's nerves
So she made a plan to eat him.
They played a game
And then she said, 'You look tasty!'
So she ate him!

**Joseph Geddes (9)**
**Tatsfield Primary School**

# Dragon

I saw a dragon yesterday
Its teeth were very spiky
I saw a dragon yesterday
Its wings made me shout out, 'Crikey!'
His eyes were very freaky
His back was very creaky
His flame shoots out and burns you.
I saw a dragon yesterday,
Maybe you will too.

**Ollie Bracey (10)**
**Tatsfield Primary School**

## Gingerbread Man And Little Bo Peep Poem

Once upon a Sunday at 5am,
The sheep ran away from Little Bo Peep.
She was running quickly along the road,
To catch the straying sheep.

Simultaneously at 5am,
Gingerbread Man went for a tiring jog.
Then at 5.05am Little Bo Peep,
Saw a pigsty through fog.

*A sheep could hide there,* thought Little Bo Peep
So she ran on ahead to get that sheep.
5.05am, Gingerbread Man saw Peep
And he had one big leap.

*Crash!*

They smashed together and fell in the pigsty
Little Bo Peep said, 'Hi Gingerbread Man.
You look very, very tasty today.'

**Elliott Griffiths (9)**
**Tatsfield Primary School**


## Autumn Senses

Autumn feels like a cold cat.
Autumn sounds like a brown, crunchy leaf
                    falling silently to the ground.
Autumn tastes like apple pie on a cold day.
Autumn looks like a leaf pile on the ground.
Autumn smells like a cold breeze.

**Jo Herzig (8)**
**Weyfield Primary School**

# Autumn Senses

Autumn smells like apple crumble
overflowing with custard.

Autumn feels like crunchy leaves
breaking up in my hand.

Autumn tastes like marshmallows
dipped in hot chocolate with cream.

Autumn sounds like conkers
as they fall down from the tree.

Autumn looks like bare trees
as they gently sing in the breeze.

**Emma Cox  (9)**
**Weyfield Primary School**


# Autumn Poem

Autumn smells like bonfires burning on a frosty morning,
Autumn sees brown and golden leaves falling from the trees,
Autumn hears leaves rolling around the playground.
Autumn feels like crispy, early dew,
Tastes like hot drinks.

**Naomi Shotter  (8)**
**Weyfield Primary School**


# Autumn Senses

Autumn smells like apple crumble baking in the oven.
Autumn sounds like birds singing in the bare trees.
Autumn tastes like hot chocolate.
Autumn feels like the warmth from a crackling fire.
Autumn looks like misty air floating over the cold ground.

**Bethany Cox  (9)**
**Weyfield Primary School**

# My Mum

My mum is kind and caring
She thinks of others too
She makes me feel warm and cosy inside,
When she says 'I love you'
She's always there to meet me
When I come out of school
She gives me hugs and kisses
If I'm ill or had a fall
Mum you're really special
I really want to say
Thanks for all you do for me
On this, your special day.

**Gemma Brock  (6)**
Weyfield Primary School


# My Mummy

M y mummy is lovely
U nderstanding and kind
M y mummy is fantastic
M y mummy understands me
Y ou are the best mummy and I never, ever, ever
    want to leave you.

**Shelby Dodd  (7)**
Weyfield Primary School


# Bats

Bats are scary, they have sharp teeth
They kill other animals and live in caves
They make lots of holes and pile up their homes.

**Mahrazul Chowdhury  (7)**
Weyfield Primary School

# My Autumn Poem

Autumn smells like cold winds on a misty morning,
Autumn looks like brown, red and yellow leaves
falling softly from a tree.
Autumn feels like cold winds blowing through my fingers.
Autumn sounds like children in shiny red boots,
splashing in puddles.
Autumn tastes like the first warm sip
of hot chocolate when I come home.

**Shannon Skinner  (8)**
**Weyfield Primary School**


# Autumn Senses

Autumn looks like misty mornings when I wake up.
Autumn feels like dewy leaves when I go out to play.
Autumn sounds like bonfires coming from next door.
Autumn smells like apple crumble coming out of the oven.
Autumn tastes like apple crumble as I eat it.

**Missy Chalk  (8)**
**Weyfield Primary School**


# Autumn Senses

Autumn smells like cold misty mornings
Autumn sounds like crunchy leaves breaking under my feet
Autumn feels like dry leaves crumbling in my hand
Autumn tastes like cold apple pie
Autumn looks like yellow and red leaves on the floor.

**Jessica Chatfield  (8)**
**Weyfield Primary School**

# Autumn Poem

Autumn smells like bonfires burning
on a frosty morning,
Autumn sees brown and gold leaves
falling from the trees.
Autumn hears leaves rolling around
the playground.
Autumn feels like morning dew.
Autumn tastes like hot honey drinks.

**Anh Nguyen  (8)**
Weyfield Primary School


# This Is My Friend

This person is glittery peach
He is a burning summer
A Legoland
And a snowy day
He is denim trousers
An interactive whiteboard
He is Futurama
And a packet of crisps.

**Jimmy Lemon  (9)**
Weyfield Primary School


# Autumn Senses

Autumn smells like bonfires in the distance,
Autumn tastes like misty air,
Autumn sounds like dying leaves falling from the trees,
Autumn feels like crunchy leaves in my hands,
Autumn looks like rain clouds up in the sky.

**Melvin Brown  (8)**
Weyfield Primary School

# Autumn Senses

Autumn smells like apple crumble
on a misty morning,
Autumn sounds like a crispy leaf
falling on the ground.
Autumn feels like a golden leaf
crumbling in my hand.
Autumn looks like a gold, brown and red
wonderland, underneath the tree.
Autumn tastes like the moist wind blowing
in my mouth.

**Rosie Clarke  (8)**
**Weyfield Primary School**


# Autumn Senses

Autumn smells like apple crumble
Autumn looks like a misty morning
Autumn tastes like a juicy blackberry
Autumn feels like leaves crumbling
Autumn sounds like conkers smashing.

**Jack Orledge  (8)**
**Weyfield Primary School**


# Autumn Senses

Autumn smells like a misty morning
Autumn tastes like apple crumble
Autumn looks like leaves floating
Autumn sounds like leaves crackling in a bonfire
Autumn feels like a new woolly jumper.

**Siân Morley  (8)**
**Weyfield Primary School**

# My Teacher

This person is calm and cool blue,
She is a hot summery day.
A cupboard full of books.
And a lovely hot Sunday afternoon.
She is a hot jumper.
A long armchair with loads of cushions.
Power Puff Girls,
And a cheeseburger just out of the oven.

**Finlaye Bartlett  (9)**
**Weyfield Primary School**


# This Person Is . . .

This person is a red mad bull
He is a hot scorching summer
He is Mexico
A cloudless day
He is a pair of mad shoes
A bouncy cushion
Harry Potter and the Goblet of Fire
He is a hot chilli pizza.

**Didier Fung  (9)**
**Weyfield Primary School**


# Autumn Senses

Autumn smells like hot apple crumble.
Autumn tastes like fresh air.
Autumn sounds like a horse on the road.
Autumn looks like leaves falling from the trees.
Autumn feels like a crispy leaf.

**Samantha Newman  (8)**
**Weyfield Primary School**

# Soft And Gentle

My teacher is pale yellow
She is a shimmering summer
A sandy beach
A brightening sun
She is the shine of my diamond ring
She is a soft and gentle cushion
She is a shallow howl
And a sour sweet.

**Carla Brenton  (9)**
Weyfield Primary School


# Shadow Black

This person is shadowy black
He is a blizzardy winter
A disco with lots of music
And a strong fierce wind.
He is a woolly coat
A couch potato
Zoro
And an all day breakfast.

**Jake Smith  (9)**
Weyfield Primary School


# Autumn Senses

Autumn smells like misty mornings.
Autumn sounds like conkers crashing.
Autumn tastes like apple crumble and custard.
Autumn feels like crunchy leaves in my hand.
Autumn looks like rain clouds thundering.

**Cameron Davis  (8)**
Weyfield Primary School

# Miss Butler's Bag

In Miss Butler's bag there is a zebra
A wooden stick to hit children with
A slimy snail
A blue new Subaru car
Some papier mâché
A tarantula, it's also big and hairy
A dead snake found in the orchard
A packet of soup and some bread
A teaching assistant (Miss Bond)
A packet of Hobnobs and chocolate digestives
Ten tickets to Majorca for her and her friends
Three million pounds
Two cats (Blackberry and Guinness)
The Concorde
Five boiled eggs
Six rashers of bacon
Three sausages
Two hash browns
A packet of hair bands
And last of all, a bundle of keys
For her front door.

**Kirsten Rayner (10)**
**Weyfield Primary School**


# My Teacher Is . . .

This person is rosy-red
She is a hot summer with a barbecue
She is Paris
And a hot sunny day
A lazy bed
Grease
And a big portion of bacon.

**Tekisha Bown (9)**
**Weyfield Primary School**

# In Mrs Blair's Handbag . . .

Mrs Blair has in her bag . . .
Six purring kittens
Two dying sunflowers
One set of car keys
Eighty stickers
A posh motor bike
Five Brussels sprouts
Two carrots
Three mouldy roast potatoes
A photocopier
A hundred pieces of paper
Two pencils
A pencil sharpener
And all sorts of paper.

**Jack Harvey  (9)**
**Weyfield Primary School**


# Miss Turner's Bag

In Miss Turner's bag there are . . .
Ten long wooden sticks
Nine leather shoes,
Eight razor-sharp guillotines.
Seven scruffy teddy bears,
Six shiny whiteboards,
Five wiggly worms.
Four blue buckets,
Three red spades,
Two black cats and
One lunch box.

**Charlotte Lee  (9)**
**Weyfield Primary School**

## Bramley Class

B ramley is a great class
R eading is fun,
A step into this class and you'll love it.
M any people love our interactive whiteboard
L iteracy is great in this class.
E verybody has some work on the wall.
Y ou'll love all the games on the interactive whiteboard.

C ome on join in with the fun,
L ike the teachers for their teaching.
A long lesson of numeracy would be great.
S ometimes Miss Odell can get a bit cross,
S ometimes she's proud of us and our homework.

**Harry Moss (7)**
**Weyfield Primary School**


## School

S chool is the best
C hildren play every day
H olidays are good
O ut to play we go
O n the field, there is a pitch
L unch is good.

**Steven Whitehouse (7)**
**Weyfield Primary School**


## Lions

L ions are the kings of the jungle
I wouldn't hurt a lion, would you?
O n their prey, they claw and kill
N ever stop a lion
S oft they are, but cute they are not.

**Daniel Gomme (7)**
**Weyfield Primary School**

# Butterfly

B utterflies are cute and adorable
U sually they lay eggs on leaves
T iny butterflies fly around
T iny caterpillars turn into butterflies
E very butterfly has patterns
R ecently butterflies are colourful
F ly, fly butterfly
L ovely and colourful butterflies are.
Y ellow butterflies are my favourite.

**Lucy Bunyan  (7)**
Weyfield Primary School


# Harvest

H arvest is a jolly season with
A pples falling from the tree
R aspberries being picked by people
V egetables all ready for eating
E at the juicy plums and apples
S treets are packed with people buying them
T rees, with lots of flowers.

**Jack Stevens  (9)**
Weyfield Primary School


# Mariah

M ariah is pretty
A nd smiles a lot
R eads well
I s aged seven
A nd everyone likes her
H er hair is brown.

**Mariah Skinner  (7)**
Weyfield Primary School

# Bramley Class

B ramley is the best
R eally fun, as fun can be
A nd our class has fun games
M um says I learn a lot at my favourite school
L iteracy is fun
E gypt is our topic
Y ou learn lots but have fun only if the class went on.

C lass is fun and full of joy
L ove the teachers!
A nd wish I could stay
S ometimes I dream that I stayed at school
S o it carries on.

**Katie Bookham (7)**
**Weyfield Primary School**


# Jordan

J ordan has
O range hair
R uns fast
D raws great pictures
A ge seven years old
N ice to know.

**Jordan Wheeler (7)**
**Weyfield Primary School**


# Daniel

D aniel is
A ged seven. He is a
N ice boy. Fun
I n the classroom
E very one
L ikes him.

**Daniel Morter (7)**
**Weyfield Primary School**

# School

Literacy was hard
Break was fun.
Numeracy, you use numbers
Spellings, you need to learn.
Lunch, you eat your sandwiches,
PE, you do exercises.
Topic, you learn Egyptian things,
Stories you read.
The bell has gone
Time to go home.

**James West  (7)**
**Weyfield Primary School**

# My Teacher Is . . .

She is fiery red
She is a blazing summer
USA race track.
She is a denim jacket
A squidgy sofa
Nutty professor

And a *big* Cadbury's cream.

**David Green  (9)**
**Weyfield Primary School**

# In Miss Butler's Car . . .

In Miss Butler's car there is 5B's homework
Her lunch box
She's got two biscuits and
An apple
Three sandwiches and
Seventeen packs of stickers and
Her cat, Guinness.

**Connor Higgs  (9)**
**Weyfield Primary School**

# My Teacher Is . . .

This person is a zingy orange
She is budding spring.
A fun park
And the rays of the sunshine.
She's a cosy pair of slippers.
A soft armchair,
The Simpsons.
She is a chocolate chip cookie
And a springy puppy.
She is the end of a long day.

**Abigail Tidbury  (9)**
**Weyfield Primary School**


# My Teacher Is . . .

My teacher is flaming red
She is a hot summer
A seaside
And a calm, stormy day.
She is a tie and a shirt,
A soft chair with cushions
Flubber
And roast potatoes.

**Ryan Smith  (9)**
**Weyfield Primary School**


# Autumn

Autumn smells like apple pie overflowing with custard,
Autumn feels like crunchy leaves dying in my hands
Autumn tastes like chocolate biscuits being dipped in tea,
Autumn looks like golden leaves, falling through the air
Autumn sounds like children playing in the leaves.

**Rachel Holland  (8)**
**Weyfield Primary School**

# Jack's Sack

There was a young boy called Jack
He lived in a sack
Which was the size of a book pack.
He liked seeing tyre tracks
He had a lot of Blu-tack
He likes Nik Naks,
He had to pay tax.
He had a map
He wanted a shack
And a racing track.

**Thomas Bullen (9)**
**Weyfield Primary School**


# My Friend Is . . .

This person is pink and purple,
She is a cool summer
Guildford
She is as hot as summer
A strap top girl
She is a bunk bed
Mary-Kate and Ashley
And a pepperoni.

**Connie Bell (9)**
**Weyfield Primary School**


# Mrs Blair's Bag . . .

Mrs Blair has in her bag . . .
Some pens,
A dinner lady
There is lined paper from a class.
She has got a hundred points
Some stickers
And a set of car keys.

**Charlotte McNamara (9)**
**Weyfield Primary School**

# In Mrs Blair's Bag There Is . . .

10 Footballs
9 Really cuddly teddies
8 Bad kids
7 Fat cats
6 Violins and two spare strings
5 Tickets to go to France
4 Mouldy buns
3 Pounds
2 Lovely brooches
1 Lovely computer
200 Stickers.

**Allison Smith  (9)**
**Weyfield Primary School**


# In The Dinner Lady's Pocket

In the dinner lady's pocket is . . .
A football (confiscated from Year 6)
A snake's body
Ten flowers
Five chocolate biscuit tins
Nineteen cats and dogs
Nine ugly horrible children
Eight aeroplanes
Two hundred stickers
Four sets of car keys.

**Brooke Spinks  (9)**
**Weyfield Primary School**

# In Homer's Wallet . . .

In Homer's wallet there is . . .
A bag full of doughnuts
Large trucks
Two computers
Five sets of car keys
Two horses
Ten dead monkeys
2,000,000 ugly children
Fifteen metal smart jugs
Twelve Euro cups
Two medals
Thirty boo-boo babies
A whole box of beer
Mega red and white wigs
Eleven elephants
A pair of smelly socks
Bottles of Still water
Silver PS2 with a scatched game
Three baby hedgehogs
Baby bodyguard
A ticket to where everyone wants to go
A set of teeth.

**James Taylor (9)**
**Weyfield Primary School**


# This Person Is . . .

This person is sparkly gold
She is full winter
A mountain peak with snow on top
And a hurricane
She is a black leather catsuit
She is a sleeping bag
EastEnders
And a frothy Cappuccino.

**Ben Harding (10)**
**Weyfield Primary School**

# In Bart Simpson's School Bag

In Bart's school bag there is . . .
A plastic bag full of rotten orange slugs,
Two new bamboo slingshots
One cuddly rabbit called Patch
A box of half-eaten candy bars
Two wasps
A full sized tiger tank
A set of Mr Burn's new black house keys
Concorde (painted orange)
One bottle of old, gone-off, rotten milk
A PS2 (black edition)
Eight of Bart's old classmates
Principal Skinner (with a new wig on)
A tattered old Santa (from 1993)
And an evil red-eyed dragon.

**Daniel Bunyan (9)**
**Weyfield Primary School**


# In Britney Spears' Handbag

In Britney's handbag there is . . .
Five matching suites,
Ten chocolate biscuits.
A pair of cats,
One smelly footballer.
Twenty limousines,
A VIP ticket to go anywhere.
Four diamond rings,
2,000,000 pounds,
Two CDs.
Six magazines and
A big wedding cake.

**Shannon Ingleton (9)**
**Weyfield Primary School**

# In Jamelia's Handbag . . .

Inside Jamelia's handbag there is . . .
Five microphones
Ten sets of jazzy clothes
Pens and paper to write her songs on
Words to her best songs
Three spare boyfriends
Ten chocolate trifles
A superstar
Two cans of Coke
A pair of boy's eyes
Pink false nails
Eight make-up bags full to the top
Her own personal hairdresser
And her own CD albums.

**Ella Purrett (9)**
**Weyfield Primary School**


# Roald Dahl's Pencil Case

In Roald Dahl's pencil case there is . . .
Five Wonka bars
Six blue pencils
A notepad
A giant peach
One Whitbread award
A great glass elevator
An ugly witch
Esio Trot
Two pencil sharpeners
And a blue rubber.

**Nathan Salmon (10)**
**Weyfield Primary School**